# Defending Yourself Against Criticism

*Other books by Jennifer James, Ph.D.*

VISIONS FROM THE HEART
SUCCESS IS THE QUALITY OF YOUR JOURNEY
WINDOWS

# *Defending Yourself Against Criticism:*
## The Slug Manual

Originally published as *You Know I Wouldn't Say This If I Didn't Love You*

## Jennifer James, Ph.D.

**Newmarket Press**
**NEW YORK**

This book published simultaneously in the United States of America
and in Canada.

93  94  95     10  9  8  7  6  5  4  3

Library of Congress Cataloging-in-Publication Data

James, Jennifer, 1943–
Defending yourself against criticism: the slug manual / Jennifer James
p.   cm.
Rev. ed. of: You know I wouldn't say this if I didn't love you,
originally published as the slug manual.
ISBN 1-55704-179-2
1. Invective-Humor.  2.  Interpersonal communication—Humor.
I.  James, Jennifer, 1943–     II. Title
PN6231.I65J36   1990
818'.5402—dc20                                          89-48771
CIP

### Quantity Purchases

Companies, professional groups, clubs, and other organizations may qualify for special
terms when ordering quantities of this title. For information write:
Special Sales, Newmarket Press, 18 East 48th Street, New York, NY 10017,
or call 212-832-3575.

Illustrations by Steve McKinstry

Book design by Ruth Kolbert

First edition

Manufactured in the United States of America

*When a simpleton abused him, Buddha listened in silence; but when the man had finished, Buddha asked him, "Son, if a man declined to accept a present made to him, to whom would it belong?" The man answered, "To him who offered it."*

*"My son," said Buddha, "I decline to accept your abuse, and request you keep it for yourself!"*

—WILL DURANT, *The Story of Civilization*

# Contents

ACKNOWLEDGMENTS      viii

PROLOGUE      ix

1 • *The Shift from Criticism to Encouragement*      1

2 • *Perfectionism and the Laws of the Universe*      13

3 • *Sticks and Stones*      29

4 • *Body Slugs*      51

5 • *The Usual Family Slugs*      61

6 • *The Youngest Stingers*      71

7 • *Verbal Self-Defense*      87

8 • *Gossip*      97

9 • *Support and Encouragement: Marriage*      105

10 • *Evaluation and Motivation: The Workplace*      113

EPILOGUE      121

BIBLIOGRAPHY      123

# ACKNOWLEDGMENTS

A thank-you to the people of the Northwest who started this "slug" collection and to all who have contributed their favorite criticisms in the interests of a gentler exchange between us.

Many people have brought grace into my life with their kind ways. You are all remembered. This is only the short list.

Linda Curtis
Edward Evans
Linda Gist
Devon James
Dale Land
Jody Locke
Norm MacFarland
Sylvia Mathews
Ellen Michael

June Miller
Alene Moris
John Paling
Amy Royer
Chris Schroeder
Dick Slater
Jan Solga
Barbara Wilson
Chris Young

# Prologue

This book was conceived in the American Northwest, where slugs abound. In case you have never seen a slug, it looks like a fat brown worm, flat on the bottom with two stalk-like antennae. It is very slimy and slips along the ground leaving a shiny trail. If you pick one up, it sticks to your fingers. When you drop it, the slime remains on your hand and is hard to wash off. Imagine a big, fat snail without a shell. YUK!

I know this because I'm a person who loves to garden. I have many times encountered one of these mollusks eating my plants down to the nub. I am also an anthropologist who specializes in urban research. I'm interested in how people survive in high-stress environments. I was a professor at the University of Washington Medical School for many years, and in 1971 two of my courses for medical students centered on cultural abuse. We are part of a cultural tradition that constantly hands out verbal slugs to people. Physicians who don't understand the impact of this on our health end up with patients who feel as sick as my plants do after a slug attack.

Culture and Illness was the first course I taught. I could have subtitled it How Your Society Makes You Sick. We are now familiar with mind/body connections, but back in 1971 it was new territory for many physicians. The culture that surrounds you—that contributes to your beliefs about yourself—can create stress, lower self-esteem, and leave you feeling bruised. My second course, Adaptive Strategies of Urban Deviants, examined how people in difficult environments survive. It is very hard to step outside your culture without significant stress. We don't use the term "deviant" anymore, but the stress of being in any way different from the cultural ideal is still with us. People who are imperfect get hit with lots of negatives. And that means all of us, because "perfect" always seems to be defined by the person handing out critical comments.

My interest in community mental health became more and more important and eventually led me to host a radio program that attempted to help people understand psychology, culture, perception, and the choices they were making in their own lives. Criticism, in all its forms, was an early topic that seemed to touch many people. I was talking about criticism on the radio under the usual labels of teasing, kidding, zingers, zaps, barbs, put-downs, when the similarity to slugs became apparent. Criticisms and slugs both come in all sizes, are hard to get rid of, and make you sick if you swallow them.

One of the best weapons against the constant barrage of negative comments some people, especially children, get is a sense of humor. If you can collect the hurts and put them on a piece of paper instead of in your mind, they lose their power. I decided to hold a "slug contest," in

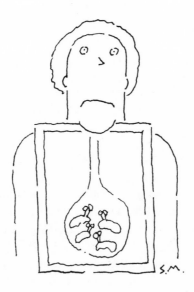

which people from our listening area would mail in their slugs. I selected the best entries and put them in the original edition of this book, which I published in 1984, titled *The Slug Manual: The Rise and Fall of Criticism.* I found out that many of these slugs were heirlooms and had been a part of people's lives for years, so our group of volunteers held burial services for anyone who wanted to get rid of one permanently and sent that person a certificate of cremation. You, too, may find comments in this book that have hurt you. You can now label them, bury them, and put your heart and mind to rest.

The first edition of the slugbook sold out almost overnight and subsequent editions still capture people who want to be able to understand and laugh at these zingers, especially when they are directed at *them.* The slugbook turned into a great "gift book" for various friends and relatives who were good at passing negatives around. With each new edition I added new slugs and more information on all the elements that contribute to the nonproductive critical mind, including perfectionism ... the need to be right ... the laws of the universe we forget ... and young zingers. With this new 1990 edition, I have completely revised the slug collection and added chapters on verbal self-defense, gossip, marriage, and work evaluation.

You may not have the closeness to slugs that we in the Northwest do, so I renamed the book to include any label you have given to the verbal assaults that are a part of your daily life. This book is a chance for you to put criticisms where they belong. Add your own to the collection and find a way to laugh. There is a temptation to give them back to the original owners, but the best option is to learn to see them coming and then duck, deflect, or disintegrate them before they can stick to you and ruin a day—or a lifetime. I owe thanks to all the people who contributed to this collection.

Enjoy this book: it is meant to make you laugh at what once stung. Use it to let go of old slug memories and sidestep new ones. Use it to understand why and how we hurt each other and how to defend yourself. Pass it on to your friends and family, with love. Remember to take very good care of yourself so that you can take care of the rest of us.

JENNIFER JAMES, PH.D.
*Seattle, 1989*

*Defending Yourself Against Criticism*

# 1

# *The Shift from Criticism to Encouragement*

*"When the going gets tough, the tough get sensitive."*

Criticism used to be constructive. In a rougher world it kept us alert to danger, and it made us conform to the group that we had to fit into in order to survive. Fear kept us working hard. We kept our noses to the grindstone. We worked ourselves to death and we survived, and so did our community. Most of us in the past were working, at least some of the time, for someone else (boss, landowner, leader, or master), and criticism was a reminder of who was in control. It is also a powerful tool in maintaining an army. It was the way we controlled our community and trained children. Avoiding censure was, to many, more important than life itself. Criticism has always been a power play, but the motives behind it have varied with the changes in our economy, technology, and survival needs.

In the past, a good parent constantly told his or her children what was wrong with them.

*"I'm just helping you be the best you can be."*

Teachers were valued for their ability to make the cryptic or humiliating remark to a student.

*"Where on earth did you get that harebrained idea?"*

Coaches were supposed to be tough, to make a man out of you or let you know you could not make the grade and were a "pussy." The worst thing for a man to be was the most feminine thing the coach could think of. Your boss was in charge and could do what he liked; pushing you, demeaning you, reminding you just who you worked for were standard procedures for establishing control.

*"Jump when I say jump. You are lucky I let you keep this job."*

People in positions of authority used criticism as a control and teaching tool, and the rest of us accepted it. After all, if your friends won't tell you what's wrong with you, who will?

*"You're always so afraid to do things."*

The interest was in toughness: no wimps, no sensitive types were going to survive in the real world. Teasing, kidding, and verbal abrasiveness were ways of sharpening the mind and the personality. Life was not for sissies; a "marine boot camp" training style would ensure your success. What the effect was on relationships was of minimal importance. Criticism was motivating. There are many areas of our culture where this rough style of interaction is still the norm.

*"He hasn't got the balls for it."*

Verbal abuse made sense when survival depended on stoicism, fear, and no-questions-asked physical responses. Whoever was in charge of the fort or the family needed to get quick reactions, and intimidation gets people to act without thinking. When the lieutenant said, "Charge!" he could not afford to have one of the soldiers ask him why or consider the possibility that to fight might not be good for his welfare. Those in authority were chiefly concerned about control and safety. Fort, classroom, playing field, work, home, all these became a teaching ground, to one degree or another, for survival in a difficult world.

*"It would be a waste of time explaining it to you."*

As survival became easier, as goods became more available, as the middle class increased in size, our psychological needs shifted. Today our stomachs are usually full. Most of us in America have adequate shelter. We have more stuff than we can possibly store or take care of. The basic economic question in this culture has changed from "Will I have enough to eat?" to "Will I eat too much?" We are now interested in quality food and quality of life. We want to be intimate, to be connected to ourselves and others, to be loved. Our communication needs are changing.

The need for safety has changed from the basic physical survival of an older hunting-and-gathering economy. We are far less likely to encounter starvation and physical danger, despite the high rate of crime and the increased risks of high-speed travel. We are far more likely to encounter and be touched by *psychological* dangers. A significant part of our population has all the necessary material goods yet is facing alienation, depression, and the shattering of basic relationships. We have changed the standard for connecting with others, for motivating our children, and for loving others. We are changing our management techniques and marriage patterns. We are now at least aware of the costs of racism, sexism, and classism. We are changing our styles of teaching, coaching, and parenting. We are learning to be not only productive but sensitive and loving. This new awareness, combined with changing survival skills, has made us notice and resist verbal attacks we once accepted as normal. Abrasiveness or cruelty is less and less acceptable in a society concerned with quality of life.

*"What a wimp."*

Energy that once might have been *enhanced* by criticism and fear is now *reduced* by verbal abuse. We are psychologically more sensitive and more sophisticated. The negative, demanding person is a problem if he or she deflates our sense of self. Such persons take energy away from us. An athlete or a child under criticism seems physically to shrink as he defends himself. His body language says, "This encounter is reducing me."

Encouragement increases energy and safety. You can see the individual become more confident and expand. More and more coaches and teachers are realizing that.

The mind and body work together! We need new survival skills to protect ourselves during this transition from criticism to self-motivation.

*"You know I wouldn't say this if I didn't love you."*

Our basic interaction mode is changing from control over people to communication with them. We want to motivate, to encourage, to empower people to use their minds and bodies rather than exert power over them. This requires a new verbal grace and awareness on our part. We once feared sensitivity—we felt it would interfere with our ability to survive; we wanted to be tough. Today we want to be sensitive. Whether we dish out and receive verbal zaps in the corporate world, the media, or the family, if we're all going to live together, a little grace is in order. Encouragement and support are far more productive of high standards than is criticism. We can accept a leader who is demanding but not one who is demeaning.

It is no longer enough to be successful. We want to *feel* successful. Success, for most of us, is dependent on how we use our energy and how safe we feel. The energy helps us be productive and the safety makes it possible for us to use all our creativity and passion. Some people walk into a room and bring energy and safety with them. They bring it in the form of acceptance and approval of us and acceptance of themselves. We are willing to pay a lot to, and give our love to, people who provide these feelings.

There are also people who take energy out of any room they enter by intimidating, competing with, and undermining the safety of others. We do not allow physical hits, so they use verbal methods. You've heard many versions of the following remarks:

"Why isn't it possible to have an adult conversation with you?"

"You're not the only patient I have."

"Here's a good book on the subject. It's written so simply, even you should be able to understand it."

"You did good—this time. Did you really make this?"

"I don't think you'll be able to understand."

"It would be a waste of time explaining it to you."

"You're hopeless."

"What do you expect to amount to? Don't you have any plans to make something of your life?"

"You don't seem to care what others think."

"You are such a klutz, you can't even screw in a light bulb."

"I like your ring. How many carats is it? Is it real?"

"I heard your daughter finally got a job. Did her father set it up?"

"It's good you made some money on that investment, but is it really safe? You could lose it all tomorrow."

"Why waste your time learning to play the piano? You'll never play like your mother."

Verbal zingers hit us every day and we're not prepared for them. Barbs are so much a part of our lives that some people hardly notice them. They slowly accumulate until you feel "down" but don't know the reason. They are like sandpaper that rubs across your sense of self slowly, until you feel hurt and worn out. Some have a funny edge, but you know where the hurt is when *you're* the victim.

We pick up these feelings everywhere: on the road, where another driver makes faces at us because he thinks we made a mistake; in parking lots or lines, where someone doesn't want to wait his turn. Many people feel free to be rude. You can find a lot of comments at stores or at work. People will stare if they think you look different or in some way unacceptable to them. Clerks who are in a bad mood will snap at you or treat you with disdain.

*"Do I have to hold your hand to get anything done?"*

*"Next.* Next! *That's* you, *pal."*

*"I'm looking for a purple dress, please."*
*"My dear, no one is wearing purple this year."*

Co-worker to another woman: *"Pregnancy has swelled your breasts. They've gone from tiny to small."*

I picked out a greeting card in a department store, found a clerk, gave her the card and some money, and she took them to a cash register out of sight. I waited and waited; other customers around me were waiting too. I decided that she had gone to lunch, or perhaps had resigned, when she came back carrying my card in a little sack. She

looked over the crowd. I waved and said, *"Here I am."* She looked at me and said, *"Oh, I thought it was someone younger."* I replied, *"When you left, I was younger."*

Saleswoman to customer: *"You could really look nice if you tried a little harder."*

*"If you were more organized, you'd get more done."*

These comments float around home and school with abandon. They are often disguised as teasing or joshing:

*"Hey, Mary, your hair looks like you put your finger in an electrical socket! Just kidding, old girl."*

*"My, you're looking so much better than the last time I saw you."*

*"You look just awful; are you sick or something?"*

*"This is my smart child, and this is my sweet child."*

*"It's time you acted like a real man."*

*"So you've read one page—a little knowledge is a dangerous thing."*

Verbal assaults are often symptoms of prejudice, intolerance, competitiveness, and distorted perception. Some people can only establish their self-worth through comparison with someone else whom they can make the loser:

My newlywed husband and I were having dinner at the home of my mother-in-law. There were about a dozen or so people all sitting around her dining-room table when the conversation turned to one of the neighbors, who was dating a girl from the same street I grew up on. My mother-in-law said, *"Well, I wouldn't think much of her, then, because every person on that street is nothing but a snob!"*

A male driver who had rear-ended me would not give me the insurance information I requested. In a condescending tone, he said, *"I'll be glad to discuss the accident with your husband."* I smiled sweetly and said that would be fine as long as I could talk with his wife!

With my mother's permission I purchased, at age twelve, a bottle of Avon's "Lily of the Valley" cream perfume. After I had it for about a week, I worked up enough courage to wear it to school. I came home for lunch from the sixth grade of a rather strict parochial school and placed some fragrance on each wrist and behind my ears, just like a big lady. I returned to school just in time to run up the stairs and take my seat. As I was sitting and feeling very grown up, smelling wonderful, a girl walked by to hang up her coat and said, in a loud voice, *"Who died?"*

*"Do you spend all your money on clothes?"*
*"Yes, do you spend any money on yours?"*

*"A new skirt? That looks like material you would use to upholster a chair."*
*"Well, come sit in my lap."*

It's easy, when defending yourself from these barbs, to get in a vicious circle of assault and countercriticism. We cannot even hear what we are saying. We carry in our head emotions and criticism from the past that do not need to be verbalized to trigger our defenses. We all hear voices in our heads, memories of other times, other comments. All of us need to review the verbal patterns in our family and past relationships to know what we are saying and what we are responding to.

Our self-view is constructed primarily of the things that we learn about ourselves as a child, plus the experiences and information that we've added since. Through observation, we learn of the ways the adults who care for us treat us. If they are anxious about the world, we assume there are things to be anxious about. If they find fault with us, we assume we are at fault. If they compete, we may imitate their behavior. As children, we are in no position to argue.

Think back over your own experiences as a child and as an adult. Think about the comments that still sting, even years later. You will understand on a personal level the power of criticism. There are many books that deal with rebuilding your sense of self if you were raised by highly critical parents. *Celebrate Yourself* and *Your Child's Self-Esteem* by Dorothy Briggs are excellent books. Jean Illsey Clarke's book *Self-Esteem: A Family Affair* also has many specific ways to encourage children and adults.

Our sense of self has a lot to do with whether we are successful or not. If you feel you don't deserve it, you may not allow yourself to be successful. You will always assume any success you have is the result of luck instead of your own hard work. Children whose accomplishments are discounted by their parents often spend their lifetime discounting their adult achievement. Check yourself, check those inner voices. Find out where the negative thoughts come from. Whose voice is it? We repeat old patterns externally and internally. If you were raised with criticism, you will find yourself seeking friends and lovers who are critical; you will criticize others as well.

Free yourself from the criticism that is a part of your

personal interactions, work, and family. Stop allowing others to put you down. Avoid negative people or being negative. Learn to ignore verbal hurts. Take good care of yourself.

# *Perfectionism and the Laws of the Universe*

*"I dream of a place for everything and everything in its place."*

Frustration, irritation, impatience, anger—the desire for control. We learn as children a terror of being at the mercy of events, situations, and circumstances we cannot control. Children of alcoholics and abusers have this burned into their soul. You want it to be different for you. But no matter how you try, how thoughtful you are, you cannot control the spouse, kids, dogs, friends. You seethe with fear and frustration. One snip of the taut wire and it will all come apart and you'll be a child again—caught.

One of the results of constant criticism is a belief that love and approval come only to those who are perfect. The people who believe this end up with an illness called perfectionism. They feel that only when they have established perfect order and control over everything will they be loved. Since perfection is an illusion, they are forever disappointed and frustrated.

## The Need to Be Perfect

Perfectionists want the house to look as though they've moved out or sealed it in plastic. They cannot recognize that life is an ongoing process, that change is constant. *She* would be happier if the other members of the family would just become neat pieces of furniture to be put on display. *He* wants the yard perfect, the car perfect, the dog perfect, and everything at work perfect. *She* feels irritated by the condition of the neighbor's lawn and the behavior of almost everyone.

You can only be "perfect" by comparison, and therefore perfectionism requires criticizing and competing with others.

> Last night I came home after receiving test results for my first exam in a college anatomy course. I was happy to tell my perfectionist husband that I received a "B." He said very seriously, *"Don't worry, honey, I'm sure you'll do better next time."*

> *"I really admire your doing the kind of work you do. My pride would get in the way."*

> My mother, who has devoted her life to keeping a house in which you can eat off the floors, has found me to be a housekeeping disappointment. I have taken many slugs, such as *"You can't get good vacuuming from an eight-year-old"* and *"If you didn't have all these plants, animals, kids, and activities,*

*you wouldn't have this dust problem.*" She spied a cobweb (an old one) in my kitchen corner one day and said, *"What is that?"* I replied, *"A science project."*

I took my well-to-do mother out to lunch. I paid the bill, left the tip, and used my car and gas. I tried to be as pleasant as possible. As I was dropping her off, she looked around my car and said, *"Isn't your vacuum working?"*

Perfectionists seem to care more for order than for people. They establish their worth only through control and scorekeeping. Their families are part of the score. Parents who never seem satisfied with their children's accomplishments raise children who are never satisfied with themselves. Perfect performance becomes confused with perfect love. Because nothing is ever good enough, the children never really feel safe or loved.

I have a friend who is in his forties. He has an older brother who is a doctor. His parents have always reminded him that he should have gone to college and been like his brother. These reminders have never stopped, even though John, my friend, is very successful at his work. John gave his father a scholarship to the local community college for his eightieth birthday. He said, "Dad, you've always wanted me to go to school. I thought if it was that important to you, *you* should go." His father immediately understood the gesture, and said, "John, I'm sorry I've criticized you and compared you to your brother." John's mother yelled from the kitchen, "John, we only want you to be the best you can be!" With some parents, it never ends. You have to make peace with yourself.

The world is full of people who establish their worth by secret comparison and overt criticism. The chickens in the yard learn the pecking order when they are pecked. The peckers in our culture are most likely to be individuals who were reared on "conditional" love: the parenting philosophy that holds that if a child cannot perform to a certain standard, he will be unloved and rejected. Rarely can a child safely debate the merits of the expectations presented to him or refute the criticism. He risks more verbal or even physical attacks. He is told, "Don't you dare talk back to me," so he learns to flinch at his own inadequacy and to avoid mistakes.

Sometimes perfectionists give up and become total failures. Some feel inadequate, but try to conceal it by demanding perfection from others. Some procrastinate, afraid to make mistakes. In extreme situations, some choose suicide in order to avoid the inevitable failure to maintain the illusion.

There are many ways to cure the problem of perfectionism, once you recognize the symptoms and want to change. One of the best descriptions of how to reduce perfectionism is from the book *Instant Relief: The Ency-*

*clopedia of Self-Help*, by Tom Greening and Dick Hobson. They list the following possible ways to make your life, and the lives of those around you, happier and more productive*:

- Rediscover yourself as more than the sum of your actions and products. Perfectionism is a way of living that overidentifies you with what you do and produce.

- Recognize perfection as an unattainable ideal, not a possible or even desirable way for human beings to live. High standards are important but we need to make mistakes in order to learn and grow.

- Strive for excellence, and when you do a good job let yourself enjoy it.

- Repeat to yourself a new motto to replace the old one. "Anything worth doing is worth doing badly." If we care about doing something, we ought to be willing to do it for its own sake, not to demonstrate how well we can do it.

- Stress your accomplishments in your mind. Stop listening to your overdemanding, never-satisfied inner judge.

- Look at the specific ways in which you are a perfectionist. Do you focus on looks, work, housekeeping? Under what circumstances are you likely to behave in a perfectionist manner?

*Quoted from pages 245–48 of *Instant Relief* (Wideview Books, 1979), by permission of the authors.

- Imagine not doing something perfectly. What are the external consequences (not your internal responses)? If there are none—as is likely—look at the self-destructive nature of your perfectionism.

- Don't get hooked on someone else's standards. If your parents are never content with what you do, recognize that they have a need to be discontented—not that you have never done anything worthwhile.

- Work at becoming less competitive. Stop comparing yourself to others as if you were always involved in an important rivalry.

- Laugh. Make jokes. Look at the funny side to life's dramas. Recognize and accept the comic aspects of trying and failing.

The healthy pursuit of excellence, the genuine pleasure of meeting high standards, is often confused with perfectionism. Perfectionism is based on the painful illusion of personal perfectability: people measured entirely by production or accomplishment. Excellence is achievable. You know it when you reach it. There is a feeling of gratification when a project is completed. You are willing to enjoy an accomplishment before you go on to the next one.

Perfectionists never celebrate. They lose sight of the quality of life in their measurement of quantity. Order takes precedence over relationships. Their expectations are more important than acceptance and love. They can see only perfect and imperfect, so they are unable to enjoy any activity or person that would leave them in between.

Once when my husband was in grade school, his class was preparing to go down the halls Christmas-caroling. As they left the room, the teacher turned to my husband and said, *"And can you just hum?"*

If you're not the problem but you live with a perfectionist, you may have to learn to hold on to your own sense of balance around others. Don't let him or her convince you to be a perfectionist too. When they criticize, gently suggest they do it themselves, hire someone, or relax. Offer to keep the things most important to them as close to perfect as you can. Ask them to set priorities (living room, lawn, car, laundry). You can be a little silly about being terribly careful with their most important needs, but do your best to compromise only where it makes sense.

Let them know you think they are wonderful. Create safety for them. Try to trace back with them the source of the perfectionism. Whenever trouble starts, remind them that you two have different values and needs. Make it clear that you are unwilling to be stressed out to please someone else.

## The Need to Be Right

*"There is a right way and a wrong way to do everything."*

A close cousin of perfectionism is the need to be right. This leads to a veritable deluge of barbs. Criticism becomes the weapon of first choice in the great fight to be right. The need to be right is usually the need to feel you are valuable because you doubt your self-worth. Therefore, you are always out to prove your worth at the expense of other people. If *you're* right, *they* must be wrong.

The time for decision is here. Do you want to be right—or happy? You can only be one. Now I know some of you are saying, "How can I be happy if I am not right?"

First of all, I am not talking about the need to be right on crucial issues such as the stress factors on bridges, the chemical contents of prescriptions, or whether you shoot someone or not. Those decisions make up only about two percent of our lives. I am talking about the other ninety-eight percent, where it is not only unimportant to be right but hard to tell who is and who isn't. Nevertheless, we still fight over it. Check yourself: What do you need to be right about?

## SOCKS

There are people who fight over the right way to roll socks. They are still nibbling at each other after twenty years of different opinions. There are many ways to roll socks. There are rollers, folders, those who turn down the cuff, and those who don't. There are those who tie socks in knots, those who buy fancy socks that snap together, and those who throw them in the drawer. There are even two kinds of throwers: those who throw them in the drawer and spread them around so the drawer will shut, and those who just throw them in and force the drawer shut.

Who is right? Well, you were taught by someone who told you what was the right way. Your opponent in the sock war was taught the same thing. But there *is* no right way. There is only your preference, which is based on someone else's preference.

A friend of mine ran into a terrible dilemma. She was a roller and her husband a thrower. She had carped for years. Then her mother came to visit—the same mother who had taught her to roll socks, tightly. Her mother was helping to put away the laundry and was throwing the socks into the drawer in a pile. When questioned, her mother said, "Oh, I changed years ago!"

## LOADING DISHWASHERS

Have you carped to your family about whether the forks go up or down in the dishwasher? There is no evidence to support the superiority of either up or down, only your preference. If you ask your family to do it right, they may do it wrong just to frustrate you. Instead, try saying to them, "I sleep better at night when the forks are *up* in the dishwasher; it's just a preference

I have." They will want to please you, once you admit you are fallible; and you won't have to hand out any more complaints.

## NAVIGATION

This starts some of the worst fights.

You're in a car. You're the passenger. Your husband is driving.

> *"Dear, did you mean to take that left turn?"*
> *"Yep, I always go this way."*
> *"Well, you know that's not the best route."*
> *"I think it's the best route. I think it's the right route."*
> *"Well, dear, we're going to be late."*

Now if you're smart, you'll stop talking right then— because there are *two* right routes, at least. There's the one that he knows, which always gets him there, and there's the one you want. But even if you stop talking you may sit there and seethe, thinking: "That fool, he thinks he knows the right way to everywhere." If he runs into heavy traffic, hits too many red lights, or makes any kind of mistake, he'll feel your wrath. By the time you get to the party or the meeting, you two may be snarling at each other.

What's the right way? There are probably about twenty-five right routes from here to there: scenic route, familiar route, errand route, fast route, checking-on-a-new-building route, etc. So next time you're in a navigation argument, if you're not driving, keep quiet. The person who's driving gets to choose the right route and you get to choose to be happy.

## CHILDREN

We often confuse our preferences as adults—which we're entitled to—with the "right" way. Children are upset by this. We say, "Do it right," and insult or humiliate them if they don't. Yet, still being open to the world, they see lots of possible ways to do things. Children are more creative, whereas adults often have closed minds and limited preferences.

A little boy called me who had this problem when mowing the lawn. His mother said, "Do it right." He was mowing the lawn his way (vertically), but she wanted the lawn mowed her way (horizontally). She said, "Do it the right way," and it started a fight. He said, "There are lots of ways to mow a lawn. You can mow it diagonally, you can start outside and mow in, you can mow it in chunks. There are lots of ways to mow a lawn." His brain hadn't yet been squeezed into a system that says there's only one right way to do everything.

Now if his mother had said instead, "John, I want you to mow the lawn this way because it's the way my father used to mow it, and it makes me feel secure," he would have been glad to comply. But she said, "Do it right," and that offended his sense of logic. Insist on your preferences if you want to. You don't even have to explain why. But don't insist on being right.

## MISTAKES

How many mistakes did you make this week? A full life requires thousands of mistakes if you plan to live up to your creative potential. When we are children, adults try to talk us out of making mistakes and we get confused. They are referring to life-threatening mistakes, but we think they mean everything.

Check how open you are to mistakes. Can you stand

it? Can you laugh? Do you shy away from things you might not do well? Do you laugh at people who seem clumsy or naive? Do you grit your teeth when someone you love makes a mistake? Are you under the illusion that everyone is watching you and keeping score? Start counting your mistakes on a daily basis and try to increase them by ten percent. This will help you to stretch and grow. A full, creative life requires lots of trial and error. Try not mentioning other people's mistakes. Take more risks; be tolerant of yourself and others. Congratulate others on the risks they take, and admire their courage. You'll have more pleasure and be much closer to what you want to be. Mistakes are the dues of a good and full life. Stretch and enjoy.

## Laws of the Universe

There are many sources of criticism in the world. They don't just come from under the rocks in our psyches; they also lurk around in our perception of the world. Some of us have an erroneous view of the way the world works, and it leaves us with an endless supply of negative comments.

### THE SUPPLIES AND TOOLS LAW

There are those of you, for example, who believe that you should be able to live in your house with your family and not lose anything. You feel that if they would just be careful and thoughtful, you would need only three combs, two pairs of scissors, one Phillips screwdriver, one nail clipper, one hammer, etc. Then, when you cannot find what you need, you run screaming around the house calling the others names and telling them you cannot stand living with people who never put anything back where they found it.

The Laws of the Universe—in contrast to *your* view—state very clearly that in the average household, over a lifetime, you will need:

> 652 combs or brushes (add more, if you have teenagers)
> 76 pairs of scissors
> 12 Phillips screwdrivers
> 82 nail clippers
> 23 hammers

Buy cheap ones by the dozen or on sale. For those of you who are trying to hide one good pair of scissors, please understand that it is impossible. You will have to wait until you are very old and living all alone. Of course, *then* you may not be able to remember where you put them. There are a number of other important laws.

## THE CAR KEY LAW

This law states very clearly that you need to have five sets of car keys. Yet many of you try to get by with only two and suffer the consequences. When, for example, your spouse loses his or her car keys you must immediately scramble and start looking for them until they are found, or you will end up in a big fight. You'll both get criticized for things that have nothing to do with lost car keys. Buy some extra sets today.

## THE LOST THINGS LAW

There is no way to live up to your full potential in life without losing lots of things. Yet there are people who believe you can go through a lifetime without losing anything, if you would just be more careful and more thoughtful. They actually believe that a child can get through elementary school without losing a jacket, but that's impossible unless the child is very repressed. A truly creative child will lose two jackets. (You *can* make him contribute to replacing the jacket.) It's important to teach responsibility, but don't assume that if they'd "just be more thoughtful" they wouldn't lose anything.

Understand and recognize the nature of stuff, and don't get mad. The creative person who lives his or her life up to its full potential will lose thousands of things. We don't have much control over lost things—only in how we perceive a loss and how we handle it.

## THE DEAD BATTERY LAW

There are varying quotas on dead batteries. Mine happens to be very high. I assume about 92 in a lifetime, so I always carry two sets of jumper cables and get big, strong batteries. When I find I have a dead battery, I say, "Oh, here's number 41." I get a friend, or a cab, to jump-start my car and I'm on my way. Once I ate a quick lunch from a roadside vendor while waiting for the cab. I saved time. I still get dead batteries—but no grief.

## THE LOST WALLET OR PURSE LAW

No matter how careful you are, assume that you will lose a few. Copy your credit cards, take out irreplace-ables, and accept fate. When a purse or wallet is lost, allow a brief panic, say, "Oh, here's number 3," and then start taking care of the loss. Keep grief to a minimum. It's bad enough your stuff is gone; don't lose your mind too.

## THE BROKEN THINGS LAW

There are, of course, those who believe nothing should get broken or spilled. Yet a creative life requires you to spill thousands of things and to break at least 7,683 things if your life is to be creative and passionate. Check your record. How do you respond when other people break things? Do you treat children differently than adults? (Children are supposed to break more things.) Do you offer a way for them to replace the item, such as working for it or having it fixed; or do you grasp the opportunity to unload a few more slugs?

There are many other laws, and you can figure out the ones that apply to your life. My favorite of all time is

## THE TOILET ROLL LAW

There are some of you out there who think that any-one in a household can be taught to put the toilet paper on the toilet roll. That's not true. The law actually says that in any given household only one person will volun-tarily put the toilet paper on the toilet roll. Now if you've got more than one person willing to do it in your house, it's because they've been carped at, and as soon as they leave home, they'll never put the toilet paper on the roll again.

I found out that I was the designated toilet-roll person in my house, and I tried to fight it. I even hired a housekeeper two afternoons a week, and I taught her how to put the toilet paper on the roll, and she nodded.

I left her notes, but in two years she has never once put the toilet paper on the toilet roll. I have, finally, accepted the Law of the Universe—*I* am the designated person—and it has brought me peace of mind.

In the end, your perspective is much easier to change than are your past, your family, other people, or reality. Once you recognize what you are actually saying to others and hear what they are saying to you, it's your choice how to respond.

# Sticks
# and Stones

**"Gee, you look marvelous! Did you have plastic surgery?"**

There are so many styles of criticism that it is impossible to catalog them all. Just being alive seems to invite some. An uncomfortable life event multiplies them. If you get divorced, hurtful comments will drift your way. Any vulnerability is a temptation for some people. Disabilities, infirmities, mistakes, pregnancy, age are all opportunities for rude and competitive strangers or acquaintances to get in their digs.

> *"You know, I would have thought you were young, except your hands gave you away."*

There are common, everyday zaps and there are "irregular slugs" that seem to come from nowhere and confirm your belief that the other person neither listens to you nor cares about you. These kinds of hurts leave us dizzy and upset. They usually come from relatives.

A friend of mine was telling her mother that she had breast cancer. Her mother, who she knew had always preferred her younger sister, replied by changing the subject: "You know your sister is such a good cook. Have you tried her enchilada recipe?"

When a man had gotten up the nerve to tell his mother that his wife had left him, he hoped for some emotional support. Instead his mother said, "I wonder what took her so long?"

On the street we sometimes encounter "rough hits." A drunk, a disturbed person, a hostile pedestrian will make a crude remark, sometimes as a defense against what they think is in your mind or glance. These stings to our psyches often create fear or overreaction. We don't let our minds evaluate the environment of the remarks. Instead, we take them personally. It helps to step back, evaluate, and let go of these barbs. Expecting that any democratic culture is going to have some abrasiveness helps too. Don't be surprised, accept some verbal assaults as normal venting of the pain and frustration we all encounter in one form or another. Someone in "the pits" is bound to sound like it.

Rush hour brings out the worst in some people. They make faces, gesture, yell, call names, bump you with their car, and lean on their horn over the slightest perception that they are right and you are wrong. If you take any of these signals seriously, you can be hurt every time you drive. If you cannot crack a joke within a few minutes of rear-ending someone on the freeway, don't go out there. If drivers cut you off on the road, you can choose how you want to perceive their actions: You can decide on war and get on their bumper, or get in front of them and slow down; you can pull up beside them and make facial or hand gestures, or you can decide on grace.

Assume that the reason for their driving the way they are is that they're rushing to the bedside of a sick child. Let them in, give them a wave—a boost on their way. Instead of anger, you'll feel soothed by your own self-righteousness and inherent goodness.

You have the option to choose your own reaction in most situations of public slight. Keep your sense of humor. The waitress isn't singling you out for trouble, she's trying to recover from the fact that the night before her boyfriend ran off with another woman or that one of her children is ill. Be gentle and the energy will change in *your* direction.

My favorite category of barbs is the well-dressed zap otherwise known as "constructive criticism." These are the "glamour slugs." Picture our slimy friend in a tuxedo or covered with glitter. This is an insulting comment usually preceded by one of these phrases:

*"I hope you don't mind if I'm honest."*

*"This is for your own good."*

*"Please don't get mad at me, but . . ."*

*"I always speak my mind."*

*"I'll be candid with you."*

*"You know I wouldn't say this if I didn't love you."*

You end up confused because you are supposed to admire them for their honesty and appreciate their con-

cern for you, while you try to recover from the punch you've received in the stomach. It is easy to tell whether you are receiving help or not by how you feel. This is an important part of the perfectionism we discussed earlier. *Constructive criticism as evaluation* is covered in Chapter 10.

Try to complete this phrase and you may remember some well-dressed zingers in your past:

*"If I didn't care for you, I wouldn't tell you that . . ."*

*"You don't like people who are honest with you, do you?"*

Sometimes these comments come in the form of questions we cannot answer or refute.

*"Why don't you act your age?"*

*"When are you going to realize you can't be a sexpot forever?"*

*"Why are you so sensitive?"*

## Heirlooms

Criticisms are often passed down through a family from generation to generation. If your mother or father called you a particular name, you will be tempted to repeat it. I remember being called "Jellybags" whenever my mother thought I was envious or jealous of someone. Every so often, that name still comes to my lips in reference to children. I have to remind myself to suppress it.

What names or labels can you remember from your past? Do you still use these names for yourself and others? What names might you be passing on? "Dummy?" "Doughboy?" "Selfish?" "Bigfoot?" "Troublemaker?" "Wimp?" "Cheap?" "Fat boy?" "Fussbudget?"

If we call someone by a label for a long enough time, he can begin to believe it. Long after the information is proven to be untrue, he is unable to stop thinking of himself as "dumb" or "fat" or whatever he was called.

Heirloom slugs often refer to characteristics assumed to be passed down.

> *"You are just like all the women in your family. You are all crabs."*

You are guilty through some historical connection that indicates you as part of the related group. Can you think of an heirloom slug that lumps a group together regardless of their individual characteristics. . . ?

> *"Isn't that just like a man."*

> *"Oh, men!"*

> *"Men aren't as sensitive as women."*

Or that uses other related people in the family to bolster the criticism. . . ?

> *"If you drink, you'll end up just like your father."*

Or that gives criticism by saying,

> *"You've always been that way."*

> *"I've been telling you to change for years."*

> *"Everyone else thinks so too."*

Sometimes heirloom slugs, if you've learned to laugh at them, are a source of humor. They become a story that is passed down through a family. Here are some "old" slugs:

My brother lives in the East. He and I were reunited after a nineteen-year separation to attend the funeral of our father in the Midwest. After making the rounds of supportive friends and relatives, we made our dutiful call on Aunt Nell. When we were leaving, Aunt Nell said, *"Just a minute, you two. I have something to say. Twelve years ago when your father retired, my son-in-law asked him if he could rent his property. Your father said, 'We'll see if we can make a deal . . .' but then he rented to someone else. The whole community has been laughing at us ever since. Now, explain why he would do that to us."*

I wish I were an artist. Can't you just see an angry slug with her little shovel, digging in the cemetery filled with little grave markers inscribed "Insults from 1902," "Insults from 1903," etc.?

After a very sticky divorce in which I lost all my prized china and silver and other beautiful possessions that I took very good care of, I remarried and brought very little of beauty or value to the new marriage. Shortly after our marriage, I was pleased to find that my husband's grandmother's silver was coming our way. When I expressed the fact that I would like to keep it neatly stored in the compartment designed for silver in my antique dry sink, my new husband exclaimed, *"Do you think I'd let you take care of this silver? Then it would end up looking like the crap you have now."* He proceeded to leave it loose in a box in his closet, where he is saving it for his daughter (an eight-year-old who lives with her mother in California).

My husband and I were teaming up to capture a mouse, when it slipped past him and escaped. I snapped, *"What the hell's the matter with you, anyway?"* I suddenly realized where it came from. I'd heard it countless times growing up. I apologized for the slug as I recalled stories of my Uncle Tom, who was great fun for us kids. Uncle Tom was once playing monster by standing on the toilet with a towel over his head. When the kids all ran out screaming, my grandfather made a trip to the bathroom and exploded, *"What's going on here? What the hell's the matter with you, anyway?"* All Uncle Tom's antics around my grandfather would be followed by that slug. So I have vowed, *"The slug stops here."*

## Time-Release Zaps

These are particularly insidious types of comments. You don't notice them when you first get them. Later, they begin to explode in your stomach. Some of these slugs have been known to continue releasing pricks for weeks and even years. Examples are hard to come by, because they are so subtle.

*"You should have changed your hair years ago. It looks nice now."*

*"You are so quiet no one can hear you or even know you exist."*

*"I saw your husband in a bar with your friend. It's nice he knows how to enjoy himself."*

*"By the way you dress, I can see that you have a hard time accepting your age."*

A mother-in-law's reply when thanked for a Christmas gift: *"Oh, do you like the bathrobe? I'm so glad. Marvin didn't like it on me."*

I found out from my sister-in-law that I was making my baby's bathwater too hot. This prompted the following from my mother-in-law: *"What are you trying to do? Cook my baby?"*

The only way to handle these slugs is to recognize them right away. Then you can either opt for the compliment and forget the rest, or you can subtly get more information. Or you can stay away from that person in the future.

Mom: *"That dress looks nice, dear, if you don't gain any more weight."*

As I met a friend of my future husband, Roy, she took my hand, examined my ring, and said, *"Oh, that's exactly like the ring Roy gave Marge!"* (Marge is his ex-wife.)

One new friend to the other, upon parting: *"Great to have met you. I don't care what they say about you—I think you're all right!"*

Mother: *"You were so pretty in high school . . ."*
Daughter: *"Why, thank you."*
Mother: *". . . and you were so friendly. You always had a smile for everyone. The boys liked you so much. You were so popular with all of them. That's because you weren't a threat to them. Boys hate brainy girls, you know."*

At a wedding reception, a friend of the groom's family: *"We always thought your husband would choose someone special. We're glad you're just an ordinary person."*

Mother-to-daughter slug (in reference to the fact that my husband is often unemployed): *"Your father and I always tried so hard to take care of you. I wish you had someone to take care of you now."* (This statement came in spite of the fact that I am a well-paid executive.)

My husband and I were both being treated by the same psychotherapist; I had just begun to have complete confidence, respect, and admiration for the therapist, when my husband said, *"Dr. _____ says you are a thorn in my side."*

Aunt: *"I see your boyfriend bought you a very expensive watch for Christmas. You must be awfully good in bed."*

Niece: *"I guess you could say that is one of my qualities. I see Uncle Bill bought you a Timex."*

In a flower show that both my mother and I entered, I did well but she did not. While I was showing my ribbons to a dear friend in her presence, my mother remarked, *"No wonder you won so many ribbons: you entered everything."*

We moved into a beautiful new home, but the builder had left the landscaping to us. As a result, I donned my oldest work clothes and spent four or five hours a day, rain or shine, picking weeds and rocks out of the mud, trying to get some semblance of order out of the mess. One day, I took off to go shopping and was on my way to the car, when my neighbor stopped me and asked if I had a new outfit on. After I said no, she said, *"Oh, it's so much more attractive than the one you've been wearing to work in the yard."*

Remark made by someone looking at a picture of me when I was eighteen: *"You were much better-looking before you got false teeth!"*

I heard this slug from my mother to my father frequently, when I was nine or ten years old, and I felt the ricocheting wounds myself. To understand this slug, you must know that my father was quite bald and not the typical image of success, despite great kindness and generosity of spirit. My mother would rub my thick brush-cut hair and say, "This *is* my mink coat."

## Terminal Slugs

These comments are almost beyond belief. They are usually associated with death or violence and their level of insensitivity boggles the mind.

You have just buried your dear beloved wife, and one of her friends mentions to you that the dress you carefully chose to bury her in was one she always hated. You or a friend are disabled, and someone either imitates you, is overly solicitous, turns away in disgust, or mentions loudly enough for you to hear, "People like that shouldn't be allowed to live" or "Can't they at least stay inside?"

One way to handle terminal slugs is with sympathy for the terrible condition of the psyche and soul of the giver. He must be really sad. You might comment, "Sorry that you seem to need to hurt people," or offer to help him with his obvious problem.

> My mother took a dislike to my son partly because he was reserved and did not display the amount of affection toward his grandmother that she wanted. She said to me, *"You should do something about Richard. You know, Charles Manson was awfully unfriendly when he was a kid too."*

> I was seven when my father died very suddenly. I did not really feel that he had died. At the funeral, I heard a woman say to a friend, *"Pearl must not have loved her daddy very much. She has not cried at all since his death."* This, to me, was the ultimate slug of my life, and I am fifty-three.

> With two babies and a husband who worked swing shift, I was not able to go to church the

expected three times a week. After my two-year-old son died, the pastor's wife said to me, *"God sometimes takes our children when we're not good parents."*

After my second mastectomy within a period of two months, my aunt said to me, *"Well, at least you're not lopsided."* My doctor's nurse said, *"You might as well die from cancer as from anything else."* My mother read the obituaries to me.

*"I'm doing this for your own good!"*

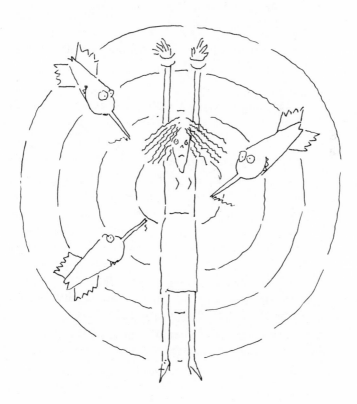

*"Why do you make me hit you?"*

*"I wouldn't beat you if I didn't love you."*

*"This hurts me more than it hurts you!"*

*"You'll thank me for this someday."*

After waiting for the birth of my first child and being fearful because my mother had lost her first, I began to despair since I was three and a half weeks overdue. One afternoon, the phone rang and it was my aunt. She wanted to know why I was so late in delivering, and she further inquired, *"Is the doctor sure the baby isn't dead inside of you?"*

Comment from a mother whose daughter has lost a baby to S.I.D.S. and has a second child with cerebral palsy: *"What's your problem that you can't seem to have a normal baby?"*

A young friend of my husband was killed in a tragic accident. His body was seriously disfigured, and his wife chose to have him cremated. At the wake following the funeral, one of her husband's ex-girlfriends came up to her and said, *"How could you have him cremated? I didn't get to say goodbye. Now I'll never get over his death."*

About all you can do is assume they feel so inadequate to say anything helpful that they just open their mouth to their own hurts, unaware of yours. Forgive them in the process of your own grief. Don't carry these stunners around with you.

## Slug Sandwiches

The "slug sandwich" is a combination of two compliments with a slug in between:

> *"You'd be so pretty if you weren't fat. What a nice dress; such a great color. It's a shame that you look so sallow in purple."* (The dress, of course, is purple.)

People often suspect you know when you are being attacked, so they try to slip the slugs past you, thinking you won't notice, or that you'll at least be too confused to catch them. You can always tell a sandwich by the fact that your stomach tightens (though you are not sure why):

> Explaining how I was interested in pursuing a Ph.D. in psychology, one of the social workers I was with said to the other, *"Gee, isn't it wonderful how a Ph.D. is within reach of the average person."*

We are tempted to give sandwiches, or the sugar-coated pill, to children: "You've done so well at this, John, but you didn't clean this corner or that corner." A better way to handle this problem is to say that he did a fine job, then wait until the next time you assign the job and add extra information about cleaning corners. Most compliments are quickly negated if they are next to a criticism. Sometimes the negative comment hurts more because the compliment opened the person up: "You're starting to look good. Have you been dieting?"

Try to separate your compliments from any negatives you have to mention. If you are an employer or evaluator, you will have to criticize because the employee or client has made a contract with you to do work or get feedback. Under other circumstances, think carefully about whether you need to mention the negative. Usually note the positive: "That's a good start." Adding more information later works.

Try out these slug sandwiches and see if you can think of any you've heard or used:

*"My son could have married someone a lot prettier, but he never could have found a better mother for his children."*

After I had been complimented on an artistic endeavor, my sister-in-law said, *"Wanda works well with her hands. I use my head."*

I still remember a zap handed me over forty-two years ago. I was a shy, sensitive teenager just beginning to make the dating scene. My new boyfriend received the following note from his very recent ex-girlfriend:

*Dear Jack,*

*No hard feelings. Dorothy is a very nice girl. In fact, her niceness more than makes up for her lack of looks.*

*Love forever,*
*Mary Louise*

College assignment officer: *"Well, go ahead and apply for the job. You've always been lucky."*

When I was in my teens, I was tall, well developed, and somewhat on the chunky side. I always wanted a dress with a full, gathered skirt, which was in style at the time. My mother and I went shopping one day for a new dress. I found a lovely floral print with a full, gathered skirt. I went into the dressing room and tried it on, excited with the prospect of owning such a stylish dress. I then modeled the dress for my mother. My mother's comment was, *"Isn't that a lovely dress! It's a shame it makes you look like a bag of wheat with a string tied in the middle of it."*

In 1974, I moved from New Jersey to Ohio, to live with a man I planned to marry as soon as my divorce came through. One day, my sister called to tell me that one of her friends lived there also and that I should give her a call. At that time it wasn't as popular as it is now to live with someone without benefit of marriage, so I told my sister I was uncomfortable letting anyone know my circumstances, and would rather not call her friend. *"Oh, that's okay, she's a whore,"* she said in a tone that said, "You are too."

Wife: *"How do you like Michael's singing, Daddy?"*

Father-in-law: *"Well, I know why he sings so well. He's got legs like a canary!"*

A group member asked the therapist what strategies he used to fight depression. He left us all slack-jawed when he answered, *"I find helping people with their problems helps me, but, of course, you don't have that option."*

*"That's a great-looking dress, dear. Too bad they didn't have your size."*

*"I really like that dress. If you hang on to it, it will probably come back in style."*

Upon returning from a really good party late at night, husband to wife: *"Honey, you looked good tonight in that dress, even though your slip was showing."*

When I thanked a neighbor for the vase she sent me for a wedding present, she commented, *"I think it's quite ugly, and I didn't want to look at it anymore."*

After many years, I invited a charming neighbor and her children to have coffee with me. I had noticed when visiting in her home that among her nice furnishings were a pair of matching lamps very much like some I had recently purchased. I could hardly believe my ears when she said, *"I have lamps like those. I can't wait to find something in good taste so that I can get rid of them."*

I've gotten control of a long-term obesity problem and have been able to stay on a reducing diet with good results. Feeling good about myself, I made a beautiful new outfit, in the color that the *Color Me Beautiful* book says is perfect for me: turquoise. I was dining in a waterfront restaurant with my tall, handsome, college-aged son and went into the restroom. As I was touching up my lipstick, a well-dressed woman turned to me and said how wonderful the color was for me. I felt really glowing inside and thanked her for the compliment. The woman responded, *"I, for one, will be so glad when turquoise comes back in style."*

*"You have a nice figure for someone your age."*

*"Your hair looks nice. It's really something, what hairdressers can do with hair."*

Comment: *"That's certainly an interesting dress! I saw one just like it at K-Mart on sale! Where did you get it?"*
Reply: *"At K-Mart on sale."*

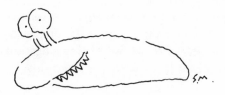

## Tiny Zaps

Tiny zaps are hard to hear but easy to feel. They are very small slights or insults that gradually accumulate.

We realize that we are uncomfortable around a particular person, but aren't sure why. We wonder if we aren't being too sensitive to his or her brand of humor or helpful comments. Tiny zingers are like the following:

*"The meat was just fine, don't worry."*

*"My son never used to be so tired."*

*"That was an adequate job you did. Thank you."*

*"I hope you'll help. You are the only one who has the time."*

*"I enjoy your daughter. Every group needs followers as well as leaders."*

Tiny barbs are sometimes referred to as a lack of tact. The usual emotion behind them is competition. People want to be very careful and subtle, but they still want to put you down. You can recognize tiny attacks by the little pinprick you feel when you get one. Sometimes you feel like a pincushion before you say, "Oh! *That's* it! That's why I feel bad."

Tiny slugs need to be ignored, avoided, or handed back just like their more obvious, bigger, slimier cousins. A stomach or heart full of tiny slugs hurts as much as a stomach or heart with one large slug.

Mother-to-daughter slug: *"You really keep a nice house. Everything is so neat. But you must remember to dust your toilet-paper holders. People notice things like that, you know."*

Left-handed compliment for my meatloaf dinner complete with homemade bread and pie: *"My, you're a fine, economical cook."*

*"Congratulations! You finally made it!"*

*"I love the way you entertain! It's so casual."*

*"Set your sights a little higher, dear."*

*"You look so nice when you dress properly. Are you wearing a bra?"*

*"I love apples in my cole slaw. Do you ever put apples in yours?"*

*"I sleep so well in a good bed. Do you plan to get a new one soon?"*

## Stereotypes

In an effort not to offend, I have left out examples of truly gross, crude, racist, and sexist comments. It doesn't take much imagination to realize that what we used to consider polite labels for groups of people we would never use now. We once believed there was one set of crude terms to be used in private for people or groups, and another set that could be used in public. We were

embarrassed if we made a slip. We now realize that none of these slurs are acceptable. Politicians can now lose an election over a label that was once a joke.

Combinations of stereotyping slugs can also be found in imitations. Someone makes fun of a person's voice, appearance, posture, or disability and it doesn't seem like fun. The issue is usually who is being hurt, should they have to handle it, and can you keep yourself out of it? We let a lot of things go by if we can keep from being personally involved. "Better them, not me" only works if you can convince yourself that we're not *all* connected. Instead, gently let people know what you feel is unkind. It's comforting to believe and feel we're all in this together when times are hard. It's worth feeling it the rest of the time too.

Some people can zap you with a hand gesture or physical expression. Think of the information in a shrug, a smirk, raised eyebrows, or the rolling of a pair of eyes. Someone's face can be a mirror in which we see ourselves reflected. Children are especially sensitive to facial expressions.

The possibilities of hurting each other are endless. Slugs can be found in all shapes and sizes. They can be brand-new or as old as your memory. They can be from those you love and from those you don't even know. All can be handled, once you can recognize them and give them a category that touches your sense of humor. You can eliminate zaps that have lasted for generations.

# Body Slugs

This may be the single biggest category of criticism. We are all raised to be very conscious of our appearance, and yet we often act as if we don't care if we're insulted. The media constantly points out the perfect body image, and it doesn't look anything like us. It is very hard, if not impossible, to feel good about yourself if you feel bad about your body. If anyone makes those feelings public via a remark, we are often devastated.

> I was passing my boss at work. He said, *"I like that outfit you're wearing. Too bad you don't have a body that looks better in it."*

When we are children, people talk about what's wrong with us as if we don't exist. They make cruel remarks about feet, noses, hair, skin, etc., as if children cannot hear. Yet children swallow these insults and believe that they are true, for years or a lifetime. A child told his feet are big too many times at age seven will always think they are big—even if as an adult they turn out to be of an average size. Adults usually underestimate the sensitivity of children, or the "power play" is so important that they don't care.

*"Look at that nose! Who's going to marry her?"*

*"If he's short like Uncle John, he'll be sorry."*

*"Don't you think he takes after Marvin? I hope he turns out better."*

*"She has terrible hair."*

*"He has enormous feet. You know what they say about big feet, har, har."*

*"She'd be so pretty if she'd just lose some weight."*

*"Oh, you're left-handed. I hear there's a school that you can go to now to get over that."*

*"Hey, here comes the whale!"*

*"My, you're looking so much better than the last time I saw you!"*

*"You've two little, beady pig eyes."*

My aunt, who is seventy-nine, has for many years been part of a Catholic contemplative religious order. Yet when I spoke to her about criticism, she remembered a comment made by a great aunt when she was seven. *"Dorothy has a sallow complexion, doesn't she."* My mother, her sister, was always referred to as the pretty one. My aunt had tears in her eyes as she told me this story, seventy-two years after the original comment. Probably no one noticed she had heard the criticism and no one else remembers it was ever said.

Weight seems to be our greatest sensitivity when we think about our bodies. We're always too thin or too fat,

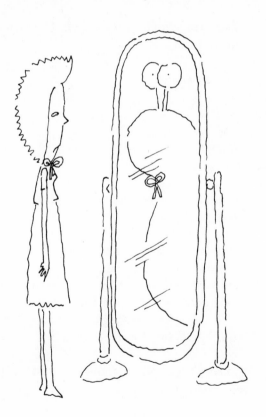

too tall or too short, too big here and too small there. Perfection will elude us forever unless we cover ourselves in white gauze and ascend. Mae West may have said, "Too much of a good thing is wonderful," but most of us have the impression that being overweight is a signal to others that we are vulnerable—and they go after us.

> Husband: *"You know, I think your thighs are getting even bigger."*
> Wife: *"You know, I think you're right, Baldy."*
> (It was the first time I had ever made reference to his thinning hair.)

*"Oh, I see you are doing the thing that you do best—eating again."*

*"My stepdaughter gave me a huge nightgown that I can't wear. It's so big I thought of you. You'll be able to fill it out."*

*"Even though you're overweight, you're solid fat, not sloppy fat."*

*"You used to have such a nice figure when you were younger. What happened?"*

After losing considerable weight, and with a friend's encouragement, one woman took the risk and wore a pair of shorts. She started feeling pretty good about it, until the friend said, *"Oh, Jane, you really are worse-looking than I expected. If I were you, I would go for some corrective surgery."*

Over a period of months I lost 20 pounds by exercise and by a careful plan of dieting. As I was struggling, I gained 5 pounds back. My mother, who hadn't seen me for several months, without saying "Hello" or "How are you?" said, *"Getting a little fat, aren't you, honey?"* I said, *"Gee, Mom, it's nice to see you, too."*

This slug was from a doctor: *"I don't know why you should have so much trouble sticking to a diet. I know both your parents, and they're both people with lots of willpower!"*

He also told her son: *"You have got to start eating better and build yourself up. Take about half your mother's food. She sure doesn't need it."*

The following was said by a fifty-three-year-old divorced man to a widow on her first date after thirty-two years of marriage: *"I used to see some of the guys in the department with their fat wives, and I always wondered how they could love somebody like that! But now I've met you and I know it is the personality of the person."* It was presented in such a way as to make one think it was meant to be a compliment. Whatever . . . it was cruel.

A friend of mine received this comment from a disliked relative: *"I've never weighed this much in my life! I must weigh as much as you do!"*

A devastating reverse zap: *"Oh, I see you've lost weight, haven't you?"* Puffing proudly, I said, *"Yes, isn't it great! I'm happy it shows."* *"It really does show, but your face has gotten so thin, hasn't it?"*

One woman's grandmother is a real pro at slugging. She is eighty-four and still going strong at it.

Her niece invited a little friend, aged eight, to join several family members, including Grandma, for breakfast at a restaurant. The grandmother noticed that her niece's friend was eating quite fast. She said, loud enough for all to hear while directing her glance at the little guest, *"Well, I guess we know who's going to have a weight problem when she grows up."*

During the first meeting with her future daughter-in-law, the mother went down the hall with her son and said in a loud voice: *"Son, why don't you go out with a small, cute girl?"*

I am a much larger woman than my mother, so I get things like, *"I feel sorry for your brother. You have been a source of embarrassment to him."* And: *"My hands are so huge I feel ashamed of them."* Then, looking at my much larger hands, she says, *"I'm glad your hands are useful."* And: *"You look like a truck in that outfit. How did you get so big?"*

I was standing at the bathroom mirror one evening at the tender age of twelve or thirteen, when my mother walked in and said, *"Don't worry, honey. If your nose gets any bigger we can have it fixed."* Up to that point, it had never even occurred to me that my nose could be anything less than perfect (and it only took about ten years for me to again love my classically chiseled Roman proboscis).

My boyfriend to me, a blond with a small chest: *"You know what's at the end of a rainbow, a blond with big boobs."*

Brother to me: *"You don't wear shoes. They're gunboats."*
Brother to me: *"Your legs look like fence posts."*
Mom to me: *"You'll never have a pretty baby. You're such a plain Jane. All your brothers* [sixteen of them] *were pretty babies."*

Our son had a few dates with Sally and one day brought her home to meet us. In the awkward moments following the introductions, we were standing there looking at one another, when Sally blurted out, *"How in the world did two such short, fat people have a tall, slender son?"*

As a woman leaves a costly beauty shop, the male owner bellows: *"Darling, when you came in you looked like 1969—now you look like 1989."*

After several months of dating my ex-husband, and quite a few times in bed together, he propped his head up on his arm after having sex and said, *"I think you are really getting involved with me, and I want you to know that I don't think I can fall in love with you, because you really aren't that pretty."* Can you believe I married him anyway?

My neighbor telephoned me one day to tell me how much she liked my hair, which I had recently "frosted." She went on to say how much younger it made me look, etc. I felt like a million dollars when I hung up the phone. A few minutes later she called back to continue the conversation about my hair. She said even her husband had remarked how nice I looked since frosting my hair. *"In fact,"* she said, *"we both agree that the lighter color is much more flattering against your skin, as it doesn't make your pores appear so large."*

One of my sister's co-workers, who had recently had nose surgery, was complaining that she did not like the shape of her nose. A person who did not know her before the surgery asked what her nose had looked like. She struggled to describe it and then, after a pause, looked around the room and pointed to my sister and said, *"Oh, it was like her nose!"*

Mother to child in carpool: *"How old were you when your nose was broken?"* (The child's nose had never been broken.)

Patty Davis, Nancy Reagan's daughter, says that no matter how hard she tries, she always leaves the house and finds out there's something wrong with the way she looks. There's a spot or a button missing, or she didn't do her hair right, or she has a pimple. She says her mother always looks perfect, but Patti hasn't figured out how to do it.

Try to unload all the body-image zingers you've picked up along the way. Most of them have long since become irrelevant to your life and your values. Stand in front of a mirror and make a list.

> thin hair
> fat knees
> wrinkles
> crooked lips
> skin that doesn't tan
> 10 extra pounds

List all the things about your body that you don't like. That is an enemies' list, because all those parts are going into the future with you anyway. Take the list and figure out which parts on it you're going to change.

You can gain weight or lose weight, or cut your hair or curl it. You can get braces or have your nose fixed. Plastic surgery has become common because of how much body image affects our success and our self-esteem. Go over everything and decide carefully what you want to do. Finally, you'll have a list of parts you cannot change or don't want to spend the money, time, or effort to change. Take each part on that list and put your hand on it. Say the following: [Nose, butt, etc.], I've let people insult you. I've sometimes joined in. You've been with me for a long time and are going to be with me a long time. Let's be friends. [Nose, butt, etc.], I love you." Make friends with yourself, all the parts, each little wrinkle or bump, and it will be easier to sidestep the negatives people try to hand you. Body blows will be part of our life until the very end, given our culture's discomfort with aging. Get used to sidestepping them and don't give any to yourself. Like yourself *now*, and be ten years ahead of your friends.

# The Usual Family Slugs

*"Wait until the world gets ahold of you."*

Relatives sometimes feel that their relationship means "no holds barred." They will say things to you they would never say to anyone outside the family. Yet we should be particularly sensitive with our family because hurts carry so much weight that they can do tremendous long-term damage. Families often carry deep feelings of guilt, shame, and fear; and the relationships are powerful and competitive. This section is a quick review of the zaps that abound within the family. (I've reserved a separate chapter for the hurtful things that children hear from parents, teachers, and peers, and there are strategies and defenses in it that you can teach children.)

The basic reasons for criticisms are always the same:

control, fear, and comparison. *We* are afraid *they* might be better than us, so we tell everyone they are worse. *We* are afraid *they* will not be safe, so we try to scare or control them. After I shared my new job description with my mother she said, "How did *YOU* ever get a job like that?"

Here are a few more family hits:

*"You couldn't possibly be good enough to be part of our family."*

*"I don't know what we're going to do with you."*

*"You can't make it on your own."*

*"When you get through 'growing up,' you'll be back."*

*"If you leave me, you'll be giving up your spirituality."*

*"You're rather plain, dear, so smile a lot."*

*"Why bother to get married again? You've failed once, so you know you will again."*

*"Well, now that you're divorced you'll be alone forever."*

*"I've forgotten more than you will ever know!"*

*"You never do anything right."*

*"I am the woman/mother in his life, and he will always prefer me over you."*

*"My 'real' father is better than you'll ever be."*

*"You've shamed the family."*

*"This is my daughter. I know you wouldn't have guessed that. She is so fat and ugly, no one thinks she is my daughter."*

*"What a fat baby! I didn't weigh that much when I was six years old."*

The only way to handle these styles of barbs or slugs is to either ignore them or agree with them:

*"You are a much better _____ than I; poor George has to live with me."*

Never, never be drawn into actual competition. There is no way your spouse or stepchild can choose between you and his or her parent without some problems. Do the same when your children bring home grandparents' comments:

*"Grandfather is probably right. I am a spendthrift."*

Your children will make up their own minds anyway, and you'll keep them out of the middle. Grandpa will have lost most of his power when the kids tell him that you agree. Stay above the fray, and keep the kids above it.

Let's say your ex-husband tells your son that you are ruining his life by demanding that he pay child support. You can either ignore it, and tell your son that these are adult matters and that he shouldn't worry about them; or you can agree that you are probably ruining his father's life:

Son: *"Dad says you want too much money and that he cannot afford to support his new family."*

Mom: *"Well, I do want enough money for us to live on and I'd like more."*

Son: *"He says you want money for a new car and a fur coat."*

Mom: *"Let's get a mink and a Mercedes. What a wonderful idea!"*

Your son will quickly see the humor and that he cannot play you off against his father. This technique also releases him from being in the middle, because your ex-husband will eventually give up passing criticism through the children when the kids tell him you agree with anything he says.

Stepdaughter: *"My mom's a better cook than you are."*

Stepmother: *"Yes, she is"* [whether you think she is or not].

Stepdaughter: *"She's prettier, too."*

Stepmother: *"I hope you grow up to look like her."*

There is no reason to fight with children about your value or compete with other adults they admire. Don't take the bait!

It is important to remember that these slugs can also go in every direction possible in in-law or stepparent relationships. Check how you handle your feelings of competition and whether jealousy leads you to criticize. Here are a few of the best in-law, stepparent slugs:

My stepmother was invited to my grandparents' for Sunday dinner. She relished every mouthful, and then commented, *"Oh, Annie, that was wonder-*

*ful. Chicken is cheap now, isn't it?"* Now in our family, whenever someone hands a criticism and we notice, someone says, *"Chicken is cheap,"* and we all crack up.

Mother: *"A loving daughter wouldn't be seeing her father after he and I had split up."*

My husband and I were discussing the care that must be taken to ensure that no grandchildren would fall into the deep end of the new swimming pool that was being installed in my mother's front yard. My mother quipped to my husband, *"You went off the deep end when you married Gretchen."*

Mother-in-law slug: *"Now that Tom has remarried and is so happy, he doesn't need to take drugs like he did when he was married to you."*

When we informed my husband's folks that we were engaged to be married, his mother's only comment was, *"What color is your wedding dress going to be?"* Being the demure young bride-to-be, I replied, *"It will be white; I don't look good in stripes or polka dots."*

My mother-in-law would look at our two little boys and say: *"Johnny is so handsome; he looks exactly like his father. Poor Jimmy looks like you."*

After the first meal I served to my in-laws, my mother-in-law said, *"I saw some winesap apples in your fruit bowl. I hope you didn't make this pie with that type of apple—I simply can't abide winesap apples."* Reply (as I whisked the pie from under her nose): *"Isn't that thoughtful of you to tell me. Now I have an extra piece for lunch tomorrow."*

During our first months of marriage, we had both sets of parents over for New Year's Day, and we served a standing rib-roast beef dinner. My mother-in-law said to my mother, *"I used to worry that none of my girls could cook, but I see your daughter doesn't know how, either."*

On the occasion of my mother-in-law's first look at my new baby, she said, *"Oh, good. I see she doesn't have her eyes too close together. Not that your eyes are that close together, dear."*

My mother-in-law entered our house after an absence of one and a half years (during which all of our free time and extra cash had gone into repairing and remodeling the house) and said, *"Oh—is that all you've gotten done?"*

Mother: *"You don't need all those children—you're too busy working all day long to be a good mother to them. You ought to send them to me. I could give them what they need."*

Here are some married-daughter slugs:

*"It's your fault my life is so miserable. You should have stopped me from getting married."*

*"When are you and Dad going to stop going away weekends and stay home and babysit like you should?"*

*"So what if you helped us financially all those times and bought stuff for the kids? My neighbor's mother gives her money all the time."*

And here are some informative slugs from parents:

*"Everyone is afraid of you."*

*"Nobody understands you."*

*"You're cold."*

*"You're selfish."*

*"You're too friendly with people."*

*"You're always trying to please people."*

During Christmas, I visited with my sister by telephone. She was telling me about her son's resolution to stop drinking. She said her mother-in-law was visiting and that her son said, *"Well, Grandma, it has been a year since I've had a drink of anything alcoholic."* Response: *"Well, now you drink too much Pepsi."*

My thirty-six-year-old aunt received this comment from her six-year-old daughter after asking her to bring her sister's coat out to the car: *"Do you ever think of me as Cinderella?"* Mother: *"No."* Daughter: *"Well, I sure think of you as the old ugly stepmother."*

My sister's mother-in-law always looked down on me for being a cocktail waitress. When my sister told her I had changed jobs and was now working at her favorite apparel store, she said, *"Oh, I didn't know Nordstrom's served alcohol."*

My mother-in-law was very proud of her ample proportions and called attention to them frequently. One day she said to me, *"How did you ever manage to keep your bosom so small?"*

My daughter was born with a cleft lip and palate. When my mother-in-law came to see her for the first time she said, *"She sure doesn't look like anybody on our side of the family."* (My daughter looks very much like my husband.)

My mother-in-law (excitedly): *"I finally found out why your sister-in-law dislikes you so. You laugh too much."*

My response: *"Ha, ha, ha, ha . . ."*

Mom to daughter: *"You should have been a boy. Look at yourself—big hands, big feet, big shoulders. You're big all over!"*

Daughter to mother: *"My boyfriend got promoted!"*
Mother to daughter: *"Well, now he's out of your league."*

Here are two regular family "guilt" slugs:

*"Do you realize how much I sacrificed for you?"*

*"I stayed with your father just for you."*

Ever since early childhood I have adored music. There was not much music around our house—my parents did not play or sing. I used to sit glued to the TV whenever I could find anything musical. When an opportunity was announced for students to take band in junior high, I was excited at the prospect of learning to play the French horn (furnished by the school). When I asked my parents for the required permission, my mother said, "No, I don't want you to take it. Music is for people who have talent, and it would mean money wasted down the line for you."

My parents came to visit us from the Midwest, after not having seen us for almost a year. When my husband and I greeted them at the door, my father turned to me and, referring to the fact that we had each gained 10 pounds, said, *"What are you doing to the two of you?"*

*"My mom says she'll quit smoking when I get my life together, so meanwhile if she dies of cancer, I'm to blame."*

Families are—ideally—a haven from the world, our basic support system. In reality, many people dread the comments they have to face when they are with their relatives. The theory that love means never having to say you're sorry is destructive: We should treat those we love with utmost kindness. There are strategies in the section on verbal self-defense (Chapter 7) that can be used to convey both caring and the refusal to be a victim of someone else's insensitivity—especially a relative's. As children we often cannot control how others treat us. As adults we can.

# The Youngest Stingers

> **"You're so ugly you must need
> to wear two bags over your head, in case one rips."**

Children accumulate the largest slime collections of all. It takes a lot of growing up, or an advanced sense of humor, to realize that what adults are saying is not always true. Kids tend to believe that adults don't have their *own* problems and are telling the truth. And parents stand by and let relatives and strangers say awful things to their children.

Under the guise of teasing, kidding, competition awakening, and constructive criticism, we beat up anyone young enough to be taken advantage of:

*"Why don't you act your age?"*

*"Look at the size of her feet!"*

*"I hope she's* smart, *because her sister is much cuter."*

*"You look like a truck in that outfit. How did you get so big?"*

*"You're going nowhere, fast."*

As a scared new mother, I remember when someone glanced at my three-month-old and asked, "Does he turn over yet?" I didn't know, so I said, "Maybe." She answered, "Oh, my baby turned over in the birth canal." My son had heard his first competitive barb.

Parents themselves often deliver the biggest ones, because they want control and feel they can achieve it with humiliation. They are merely repeating a pattern they learned as children. They may feel competitive, or they just don't know the difference between encouragement and criticism. We have such a fear of failure as parents, we care so much that we are overzealous and may hurt our children. But we may feel, too, that we will keep our child safe if we push him or her with negatives. We confuse perfectionism with high standards. Children who are *encouraged* are more likely to perform to the best of their abilities than children who are *criticized*.

Parents can also be so afraid that their children will think too well of themselves and become conceited that they neither compliment them nor allow them to accept compliments:

*"She may look good to you, but you should see the way she keeps her room."*

*"He could do much better if he wanted to."*

*"We can't imagine that he'll ever amount to anything."*

Many of the hardest hits come from parents trying to discipline or scold their children. Imagine a four-year-old who walks into the kitchen and sees a bowl of cherries, her favorite thing. What's the normal impulse? To eat them all, of course! Her mother comes in and sees the little girl stuffing cherries into her mouth. "Oh, Julie, I'm so disappointed in you. I didn't know you were such a selfish little girl." As the child begins to shrink in shame, Mom delivers the next blow: "You are a little pig, a selfish little pig. Nobody likes a greedy-guts."

There are other ways to teach kids to be unselfish without shaming them: "You sure love cherries, don't you? Well, so do I, but if you eat them all the rest of the family won't be happy about it. I'm going to put the rest away, since you've had your share." The child gets the same message but without being wrapped in a judgment she doesn't know how to handle or defend herself against.

Parents deliver giant prediction zingers as a way of

exercising power and putting a child down. They don't realize that the kids may follow their lead; they will believe what the parent said, and zingers can become self-fulfilling prophecies.

*"With a face like that, you'll never get married."*

*"Anyone who sees your room won't want to be your friend."*

*"You are always a problem."*

*"You're on your way to hell in a hand basket."*

*"I suppose you'll never be able to do any better."*

*"I'm very disappointed in you."*

*"I can't count on you."*

*"You'll be the death of me yet."*

*"You're driving me crazy!"*

Mother to her ten-year-old daughter, who has just asked her, "Mama, am I pretty?": *"No, honey, but you're going to be a nice woman. Not pretty, but nice."*

When I played basketball and lost my first game, my dad walked up to me and said, *"Hi, loser."*

I had been waterskiing for a long time. I asked my dad to teach me how to ski on one ski. He turned to me and said, *"I bet you ten dollars you'll never make it."*

Relatives, teachers, neighbors, coaches, and even strangers hand slugs to kids in front of their parents, and no one does anything about it.

*"You couldn't hit a ball if your life depended on it."*

*"He's awfully small for his age."*

*"Can't you do anything with him?"*

*"You are invited, but don't bring him."*

*"What happened to her face?"*

*"You're not the only student I have."*

*"Don't you ever consider anyone else's feelings?"*

*"Why aren't you more like your brother?"*

Parents and other adults need to listen to the actual meaning of the statements they make to children. An adult usually has more resilience than a child and will not take the comment literally. The value of self-esteem—a sense of one's child's own worth—outweighs our need to verbally put him down.

Another tough situation, especially for teenagers, is the verbal abuse they get from each other. Peers will tease about looks, clothes, intelligence, family, personality, "cool," coordination—everything about image. They will bark as you go by to let you know they think you're a dog. They'll suggest you wear a paper bag over your head.

They do it because they are scared. They've been raised on constant comparison and competition, and every day they must jockey for position to feel that they have any value. Kids who *deliver* a lot of criticism are kids who have been *given* a lot of it. It's natural to try and unload some on anyone within striking distance.

Here are samples of the current zappers in the middle-school set. Add your own, if you've got a collection:

*"Nerd!"*

*"Geek!"*

*"Your hair doesn't look bad for a change."*

*"Hey, zithead!"*

*"Don't you have any other clothes? You always wear the same thing."*

*"Wow, you're almost as cute as your dog!"*

*"Hey, tinsel teeth!"*

*"You smell!"*

*"What are all those spots on your face? Been eating with a fork again?"*

We all recognize big, mean comments like "I don't want you" or "I wish I'd never had you." But even very young children pick up barbs. One teacher asked first-graders what hurt them, and this is their list:

*"When older kids laugh at me and tease me because I'm little."*

*"When you're talking and they turn their back on you."*

*"When they say, 'Nani, nani,' or say, 'So!' "*

*"Sometimes they'll play with everyone but me."*

*"When they tell jokes or secrets about you."*

*"Being called 'baby.' "*

*"They make up names for me that are nasty."*

*"Sticking tongues out or thumbs down."*

*"When they roll their eyes to show they don't like you."*

Very perceptive for children who are only six or seven! Third-graders were asked at one school about verbal slugs and how to turn them into butterflies. Their examples were wonderful. We might wish adults could be as perceptive:

> "When my sister starts following me, I sometimes push her. But after I've thought about what I did, my heart tells me I'd better say I'm sorry."

> "I don't like it when kids call me 'Bucktooth,' 'Beaver,' and 'Chipmunk.' But I know when I'm older I can get my teeth straightened."

> "I hate when people say 'Shut up' to me, because it makes me want to say it back."

> "Slugs that we turn into butterflies are when someone is about to beat you up. You say nice things to them and they don't beat you up."

> "It's like when you're mad at somebody and you make up."

> "When you take something that is someone else's and they know, and then you tell the truth and you're friends again."

> "If you're going to say something mean to someone and you say something nice to them instead."

Criticisms follow children all the way through school. These are from fifth-graders:

"When people think you're dumb because you come from a family with problems, or when you come from another country."

"When you're doing something that you don't know how to do and your friend says, 'I can do that better than you.'"

"When no one wants you on their team, it's a real bad hurt."

"When the friends you always play with say you can't play, you always cry a little."

"When people try to make you do what you don't want to do."

"When I am sick and miss something and people tell me how much fun it was and say I shouldn't have missed it."

"When someone always says something rotten and then says, 'Just kidding.'"

"Someone told me, 'If you were any worse at sports, you'd have to be in the Special Olympics.'"

"You're so black I can't tell you from the chalkboard."

"If you touch me, I'll have to be quarantined!"

"Every child in class almost was going skating. A boy who I liked said he wouldn't go if I went."

"Hey, geek!"

*"I was walking and I had short pants on, and someone asked, 'Where's the flood?'"*

*"I was looking at some clothes and a kid said, 'Your mom and dad don't have enough money to buy that sweater.'"*

*"I was over at a friend's house to spend the night. We were in a fight and she said to me, 'You jerk! I never liked you, anyway. I just said I did so I wouldn't hurt your feelings.'"*

*"A classmate said that I should have been kidnapped. It hurt me because it was so frightening."*

*"I was talking to one of my friends and I started my sentence 'I think . . .' and she said, 'That's a first,' and went off laughing."*

*"Once, when I was going to my classroom from the bus, some kids started to laugh at me and I couldn't figure out why. They said, 'You're ugly and your clothes don't match!'"*

*"I was walking by the spider bars and a boy was talking to all the 'cool kids.' All of a sudden he screamed, 'What's bigger than her lips?' I almost cried."*

*"A kid at school said to me, 'You're a smelly, dirty, no-good, skinny weakling!' All I was doing was playing softball."*

*"They call me 'Four Eyes,' 'Brace face,' 'Blubber Body,' too,*

*Say I'm so ugly that I belong in the zoo.*
*Being called names makes me feel so bad.*
*That I wish they'd just stick with the name that I*
  *have."*

*" 'Cause I can read music and I can do math,*
*Make soap monsters when I take a bath,*
*Why should how I look make them all laugh?*
*It's true that it really, really, really, really hurts when*
  *they do."*

*"They call me 'knock-kneed,' 'baby-faced,' 'dummy,*
  *dumb, dumb,'*
*Say that I'm such a wimp that I can't even run.*
*Why can't they be nicer and just let me be,*
*'Cause there's lots of good things about people like*
  *me!"*

Teenage slugs make up another category. I cleaned these up, since using "dirty" words is part of their style.

*"You get such good grades. Do you cheat?"*

*"I wish I had your feet, then I could ski for free."*

*"When you were born, they slapped your mother."*

*"Was your nose broken?"*

*"Your socks match your earrings."*

*"Still riding the bus, huh?"*

*"If I were you, I wouldn't have done that."*

*"You could have found someone better than him."*

*"You look a lot like your mom. She's got a weird face."** 

Helping children to see the humorous side of criticism, as well as the weakness behind the remarks, makes a big difference. Some classes and families hold "zap" contests. Their children learn that everyone is the butt of rude and cruel remarks: they hurt, but we can laugh at them. After such a contest there is an immediate jump in the kids' self-esteem. They hurt less, and fewer kids are willing to hand out barbs, since they know they can get caught with

> *"Wow, that's a winner, that's a hit of the month. Let's turn it in for a prize."*

Just keeping a record of the best slugs helps. When Dad tells you how awful you look, get out a notebook and ask him to repeat it so you can write it down for your collection. Criticism is toxic. Get it out of your head and on to paper. If he asks you why you're keeping a record, tell him it's for a contest—or for your therapist, if you need one later.

Keep a positive/negative notebook page for a criticizing teacher or classmate. Every time he or she makes a remark to you, put it down as a negative or a positive. Make it obvious that you're keeping a list. Check their good days and bad days with a graph.

Understand, above all, that the idea is to put you down. The persons giving you verbal abuse have a prob-

*Thank you to the students and teachers at McGilvra School, Issaquah Middle School, and Marysville-Pilchuck High School (Washington State).

lem. Maybe their parents hurt them or they are scared. How you handle it determines how you feel and is up to you. It doesn't help to fight back: the remarks will multiply and do both of you in. Here are some comebacks that work:

*"You sure know how to hurt a guy."*

*"Amazing, but true."*

*"You're right, and it's going to get worse."*

*"No-o-o! Really?"*

*"Would you put that in writing for my collection?"*

*"That was supposed to be a secret."*

Use your sense of humor by making anything and everything into a joke:

Slugger: *"You're so ugly you need to wear two bags over your head, in case one of them rips."*

Response: *"It always helps to be prepared"* or *"Ohh, I'm glad you noticed."*

Slugger: *"You'll eat anything. You are the worst slop can I've ever seen."*

Response: *"It's great to be number one"* or *"I'm a real pro."*

Sometimes it helps—especially with adults—to let them know that you know they are out to hurt you:

*"Thanks for the confidence booster."*

*"I love getting compliments."*

*"Well, it's been fun talking to you."*

*"Ouch!"*

*"That hurts!"*

*"Direct hit!"*

To survive well in this world, you need at least three skills: flexibility, a sense of humor, and self-esteem. There are hundreds of ways, using these skills, to see a slug coming and send it into outer space. The important thing is to know that some people have book bags, pockets, briefcases, and purses full of them—and that they'll hand them to anyone who appears to be a taker. As soon as they know you are onto the "game," they will leave you alone: nothing hurts a critic more than being caught in the act. However, if your parent or teacher is the criticizer, be careful and very diplomatic. When you take care of yourself, they lose a little power and may shift to other power styles.

Check your attitude and your own slug-throwing tendencies so that you can save your energy and enjoy your life. Why do to *someone else* what you know would hurt *you*? When you zap people, everyone loses!

# 7

# *Verbal Self-Defense*

*"A kiss or a hug, but never a slug!"*

Learning to catch and defend yourself against verbal assaults makes your life easier and more pleasurable, and gives a big boost to your self-esteem. Instead of finding your confidence and contentment worn away by verbal barbs, even tiny ones, you begin to realize that the problem is not yours. The *other people* have serious social and self-worth problems, not *you*. Deflect the attacks back to where they belong. You'll not only help yourself, you'll help them to see what they are doing and learn to stop it, or at least they'll search out new victims.

These are the basic defenses in sidestepping zaps. The first step is understanding what is going on, but then you will need a variety of approaches. Applying the right strategy depends on which response works best in the particular circumstances you are in.

**Know when you are under attack.** Listen to your stomach. It will always let you know when you are attempting to swallow slugs. If they are small, sometimes it takes a few for you to feel queasy or tense. If your mood changes suddenly—you were feeling fine, and now you are a little depressed—find out why. Go back over the last few minutes of conversation and see if you can find the stinger. Sometimes we don't figure it out until a day or two later; that is particularly true of time-release zaps. But it's never too late to set up a defense, once you recognize you've been hurt.

**Check what kind of attack you are facing.** Is your mother or some other relative just repeating the family pattern without much thought, or are they going after *you* directly? Is the issue competition with a friend, relative, or stranger? Are you dealing with an abrasive cultural style that favors verbal gamesmanship and putdowns as a way of keeping people on their toes? It may be offensive, but is it serious? Is the person upset for some reason that is obvious? Is this a work situation; i.e., an evaluation? Do a quick check of the nature of the attack.

**Avoid personalizing the conflict.** This is not your problem unless you want to believe that every criticism somehow has your name on it and is therefore an accurate reflection of your worth. If that's your belief, you may need to go to a counselor for some intense work on self-esteem. Generally assume that these kinds of remarks bear no resemblance to you or to reality. Don't worry about not noticing some of your imperfections.

Most of us are hard enough on ourselves without letting everyone else wreak havoc on our self-image. If the same issues come up over and over again, you can spend some quiet time evaluating what part *you* might be playing. If a number of people tell you that you talk too much, try to listen to yourself.

**Analyze the remark.** In *The Gentle Art of Verbal Self-Defense,** * Suzette Haden Elgin suggests dividing up an attack into its parts and responding to each of them, without getting yourself involved as a victim. Here is an example:

> *"Even a woman should be able to understand this."*

Respond to the "even a woman" part as if it did not refer to you:

> *"When did you start thinking women were inferior?"*

And then there is:

> *"If you loved me, you would lose weight."*

Dodge the slug by asking:

> *"How long have you thought I didn't love you?"*

Examine what is said as data before you get your emotions involved. Don't take the bait the first time—if you can possibly avoid it.

**Look beneath the insult.** What is happening to the person trying to hurt you? What is going on at this

*New York: Dorset Press. 1980.

moment in his or her life? When it is someone close to you, there should be a way to look beyond the attack. Most people are not upset for the reason they think, or want to project. They are usually afraid of something when they try to score against another person, especially if it is someone they love. If you can't figure out what they are afraid of, then ask them.

**Evaluate for prejudice.** Sadly, we live in a culture that doesn't always support compassion, tolerance, and empathy. If you think an insulting remark sounds racist, sexist, classist, or like any other stereotype, you are probably right. The best reply is, "I don't think or feel that way." This is a negative reply, in a sense, but letting racism go by is far worse. Try to be diplomatic, use your humor, be gentle, don't be self-righteous—but always counter such remarks whether you are among friends, at a dinner table, or in a public meeting. Some people may think you are a pain in the neck, but you either are a "citizen of the world" or you are not.

Once you have a framework for action and a sense of your own worth, you can choose a strategy that fits the situation. Make the defense fit the attack. Try never to get into a verbal loop that increases in intensity. Exchanging insults can easily get out of hand and cause a hurt that is very difficult to repair, or the exchange can even result in a physical assault. I was a consultant in a sexual-harassment charge in which the woman had tried fighting back by getting as crass as her harasser. He was so stunned that he hit her.

> Co-worker: *"The last time I saw a face like yours, it was on a cow."*

Reply: *"The last time I saw a face like yours, it was under a horse's tail."*

I know it's tempting. I know you have a fine wit. But don't do it!

**Bury the slug.** If you are strong enough, just notice the remark, recognize it isn't yours, dig an imaginary hole with your foot, drop it in, smooth it over, and let it go. Breathe deeply and check your stomach. When you put a barb down, you may feel the residue (remember, the slug leaves slime on your fingers), but this is still a lot better than holding on to it. The ability to forgive and let go is one of the most important survival skills any of us has.

**Give it back.** Be as direct as you can and send the remark right back:

*"I'm sure you didn't mean to insult me."*

*"Is there any reason you would want to hurt my feelings?"*

*"Are you aware how that remark might sound to some people?"*

Or you can ask the slug sender to clarify:

*"What did you mean by that?"*

*"I want to make sure I understood what you said."*

If you ask people why they gave you the hit, they may get angry: people who criticize have a lot of hurt to unload and are afraid you will notice. Fear usually hides itself in anger and irritation. Sometimes they will switch to *tiny* slugs, hoping you won't catch them. My mother used to put ground-up liver in my orange juice so I'd be healthy. It would sink to the bottom. I always thought there was something in the glass, but I wasn't sure until it was too late. Little slugs are like that.

It's not easy to hand stingers back, because people are embarrassed. Your mother may say, "I'm not hurting you, dear. I'm just helping you to be the best you can be." Or friends or relatives will say, "If *I* don't tell you, who will?" or "I'm just being honest."

Tell them not to bother; that you are an adult and can get all the personal information you need in more comfortable ways. They may be insulted at your defense, and you can just let them vent their frustration. There is no reason to argue once you've made your point. They may want to have a tug-of-war with a slug, but you know how messy *that* can be.

**Register it.** Let them know you noticed the remark but have decided not to respond to it directly. Why bother? When at a party, if your spouse or friend zaps you, just go, "Ohh . . ." as if something surprised you; or wipe an imaginary spot off your shirt or dress. Then go on with the conversation. If someone asks what you are doing, just comment that you thought something hit you but you must have been wrong. When *they* know *you* know, criticizers are much more careful.

You can also get out a notebook and write it down. This works great for adults (as well as for kids, who don't want to offend teachers or parents beyond a certain point). Ask the slugger to repeat the remark so you can record it correctly. If he or she asks for an explanation, just say:

*"I'm writing a book."*

*"My therapist likes me to keep records."*

*"I'm going to enter this in a contest."*

*"I want to keep track of my good days and bad."*

Make up your own retort until you have one that fits.

**Extinguish it.** Blink your eyes, yawn, look away. People hate to think that what they are saying is boring to you, when they had hoped to intensify your attention. You can modify negative behavior by being disinterested in it.

**Drape it over you.** Ahh, a slug stole, a zap scarf. If you have a sense of humor, just agree with everything they have said:

Slugger: *"You've gained weight, dear. Aren't you about 20 pounds overweight?"*

You: *"Yes. Actually, it's closer to 25. Terrible, isn't it?"*

Slugger: *"Aren't you going to do anything about it?"*

You: *"Probably not. If I were, I would have—and I didn't, did I? I'm just going to be fat for a while."*

Go along with whatever is said until the other person gets bored. Take the power out of the remark. It only has power if you *grant* it power.

Criticizer: *"This house is a mess!"* [Translation: It's not perfect.]

You: *"Yes, it is. It was even worse yesterday."*

Criticizer: *"Well, aren't you going to do something about it?"*

You: *"Probably not. I mean I didn't, so I doubt it."*

Criticizer: *"You could learn to be a better house-keeper."*

You: *"Isn't it time we faced reality? I've tried, and I think I'm just not good at it."*

Criticizer: *"It's very hard for me to see you live this way."*

You: *"Yes, I know, I worry about you. Maybe we could hire some help, or you could help, or your mother could come over."*

Criticizer: *"It just does no good to talk to you."*

You (thinking): *"Right!"*

**Resist:** Write a letter to the criticizer politely saying that you are not going to absorb any more of his re-marks. Talk to criticizers you live with and inform them of your new resolution. When they criticize you anyway, ask them why they want to hurt you; walk away; close your eyes; deflect the criticism by yawning. Also, you can tell them that you'll allow only one criticism per telephone call; that you'll hang up the telephone after they give you two (if it's someone you love, say "I love you" just before you hang up). And that you'll allow only one criticism per letter; when you get to the second one, you'll just cut off the rest of the letter and mail it back (they'll learn to stop, or they'll fit a lot into one sentence).

A woman told me her husband only criticized her in public. She began to carry a small towel. She put it on her head, covering her face, whenever he made a hurtful remark. He was so embarrassed by the towel that he stopped.

**Record slugs for future reference.** Begin a list to-day, and keep track of where your barbs are coming from. Start a notebook to write them in and give them a 1 to 10 rating. Which hurt the most? Just writing them down will give you a perspective. You could have a "slug of the week" contest with yourself. You'll learn about where the barbs are coming from and whether they are increasing or decreasing.

**Catch them even if it takes awhile.** Sometimes you won't identify the zap you've been given until a few hours later. As soon as you do, throw it away. But keep track of who hands you criticism, and stop the slugger. Find a way to deflect the slugs, or stay away from the person. If you cannot avoid him or her, start working on handing the worst stingers back.

**Set up signals.** One family stopped nasty remarks around the dinner table by using a bell like the one for calling servants. Whenever anyone got put down, he or she reached for the bell and rang it. Even the grandfather, a longtime slug specialist, realized he couldn't get away with it anymore.

You will be able to come up with your own strategies, especially if you let your sense of humor loose. Remember that this is important business if you believe in taking care of yourself. When there is an intent to hurt (there always is in a verbal assault), it is not a game. It is not kidding, teasing, or "just fun." Watch out that you don't feel guilty for finally defending yourself. Criticizers usually pick on people they think will put up with it, so you probably have a bit of the martyr in you. Maybe you are too willing to be a victim.

We repeat old patterns. Feelings and actions that are familiar feel safe even when they are negative. If you were criticized a lot as a child and dutifully swallowed it all, you will look for companions and lovers who make you feel at home. It's time to change.

# Gossip

Gossip can be a form of criticism that is indirect: hurtful remarks gradually wend their way toward you and you may never know the source. It can also be a direct hit. People may only pretend to have heard a remark elsewhere in order to disguise their desire to criticize you, or they will say that "everyone" is talking about you and agrees you have a problem. What can you say to defend yourself if you don't know the source of a comment or if everyone is somehow unanimous in criticism of you?

Gossip and rumor will be with us forever. It's interesting and vicarious entertainment that we couldn't get any other way. It would be very difficult for any society to get along without exchanging informal information about people and events. We want to know all sorts of things about each other. We want so much to understand each other's behavior. Talking about ourselves and others adds emotion to conversations. It is not inherently negative.

It's helpful to understand the informal role that personal information plays in our society. Gossip is a way of building trust and intimacy between friends and learning more about yourself. It is a way of keeping up with people we don't see often. If we knew only what people wished to reveal directly, our ability to understand them and respond would be much more limited. We learn a lot from analyzing our response to the behavior of others. We make connections through gossip. We might hear someone is available to date again and we call, or we hear he or she may be unhappy or ill and needs our help.

Gossip is also a way for a society to exert informal justice. We don't like people getting away with things. Knowing they might be talked about keeps some people in line and reaffirms social values. Before legal codes developed, social ostracism was the main force available to control behavior short of physical assault. Gossip is a form of communication or protest when more direct means seem unavailable or dangerous. If you know someone is abusing his or her spouse or children and you talk about it, someone else may take action. It gives us a sense of justice, or at least the feeling of unloading uncomfortable thoughts and feelings.

Men occasionally rail against the gossip of women because men and women gossip in different ways. Men usually talk about business ethics or success and about public behavior. They believe they are only making accurate statements or unemotional comments. Women sometimes discuss private behavior, which is seen as "small" or negative. We hear horror stories of women passing rumors around about face-lifts or about a marriage that is in trouble; we respond in a very different way to rumors of someone being fired, a political liaison, or a corporate takeover.

AFTER DINNER SLUGS

The important thing to understand is the difference between good and bad gossip, rumor and fact—regardless of the person or subject involved. Good gossips know a lot, but are careful to share only information that is appropriate. They are rarely indiscreet and they regret hurtful mistakes. They are willing to apologize, and they can keep a secret. They like to keep up with the news, not dig for the dirt. Anyone who claims never to gossip is either lying or uninteresting. Good gossips follow the rules. They do not carry malice in their hearts or mouths. When they feel hurtful toward someone, they keep quiet or tell only their best friend.

- Don't gossip to get attention or fill in a conversational lull.

- Don't lie or exaggerate information.

- Don't invade someone's privacy regardless of how "public" you think that person is. The *National Enquirer* does enough of that.

- Don't tell someone things you know will hurt that person.

- Keep your promises of secrecy; be trustworthy.

- Don't gossip all the time, and with everyone. Use moderation to keep your own life in balance.

- Be thoughtful and discreet; keep your own secrets if you are not prepared to have them shared.

- Be considerate in talking about the lives of those who are close to you. Your friends and family may not be as open as you are.

- Assume *you'll* be gossiped about too.

Public-relations experts often say that it doesn't matter whether the publicity is good or bad, just as long as people are talking about you. In some cases it may be true. Remember, if no one is talking about you it is because your life is not interesting to them, not because you are perfect. If lots of people gossip about you, think of all the entertainment you provide and how important you are. Most of us try to contribute in whatever way we can. We'll have interesting stories in our old age.

When someone gossips about you and you don't want to be talked about, there isn't much you can do, even if it hurts. Rarely does it make sense to try to find the source of a piece of gossip or to fight back. Someone who wants to hurt you can always find another way. It's a grin-and-bear-it situation. You can limit bad gossip about you by either telling everyone everything or sharing very little. A middle ground is to take risks with trusted friends and pay the price if you're wrong. It is probably worth it for the pleasure of sharing. These rules may protect you if you fear being hurt:

- Never tell anyone secrets about your involvement in criminal behavior. This seems obvious, but some people talk about their tax loopholes or purchase of stolen goods with no idea of the possible repercussions. It's best to be honest; but if you don't want to be, keep quiet.

- Be very careful when sharing information about your infidelities or anyone else's. There are situations where letting a good friend know what others know about a partner's infidelity is a kindness. It is not an easy decision.

- Never tell anyone negative things about your lover's sexual performance.

- Don't say hurtful things (even if they are true) about friends and relatives unless you are *sure* your motivation is positive. Your stomach will tell you what you are doing.

- Be very careful with gossip at work. Always assume that someone will tell the boss.

At the television station where I worked, the building was being redecorated for a special visit of the national network anchorman. It was exciting, and many of the upper-level managers were taking it very seriously. I overheard a joke that they were replacing the toilet seats in the men's restrooms but not in the women's. The theory was that the anchorman would not see *our* toilets. I repeated the comment in front of some colleagues, never dreaming that one would report it to the president of the company. I was called on the carpet and told to be more positive. It was hard not to giggle, but I used common sense and kept quiet—this time.

Someone who has betrayed your confidence before will probably do it again. Ask your friends not to repeat bad gossip about you to you. Tell them you don't need to know. If they tell you anyway, they may not be friends, and they are certainly giving you a slug, even if it's secondhand. They may like stirring up trouble between you and others.

A woman I worked with, liked, and trusted told me for years that another woman didn't like me. She told me a number of stories about this woman sabotaging our plans or saying critical things about my work. For years I hated the woman, even though I hardly knew her. Eventually I decided it was silly, and took her out to lunch; we realized that we were both being told negative stories about what the other had said. Our feud was created out of what others saw as a natural competition and gossip. We realized we liked each other, laughed, and agreed not to listen to any more stories.

Avoid becoming obsessed with an attack on your integrity or family. If the stress of being gossiped about stays with you more than a few weeks, get some help to put it in perspective. Don't let low self-esteem make you accept gossip as a valid indication of what people believe about you. Negative information can make us irrational. Take a deep breath.

Try not to attack whoever you think is the gossip. It is almost impossible to trace rumors. You could be wrong, and the person may deny it anyway or be more motivated to hurt you. If it's a relative, be careful not to get into a family feud. It could last a lifetime. If all else fails, it may be worth it, with a family member, to seek counseling to uncover the real issue.

There can be interest and pleasure in sharing the bits and pieces of our lives with others. It can bring us closer and teach us a lot about life. But we need to know ourselves and our motivations in order to keep a decent balance between pleasure and pain. Listen carefully to yourself. Your stomach will let you know when you've tipped the balance.

# Support and Encouragement: Marriage

*"I'm only telling you these things to help you."*

*"You never consider anyone else's feelings."*

If you don't get to criticize anymore, if you refuse to be a victim of verbal attacks, how can you inform, correct, express preferences, evaluate, and learn? People do need a constructive nudge now and then. We all want high standards in our children and our spouses. How can we get them without criticism?

*"My, look at all the dirt you have in this corner!"*

*"I'll never be able to trust you again."*

Remember, first, that love contracts are different from work contracts. Work evaluations are discussed in Chapter 10. When you love someone, the goal is to deepen that love, to share a life, to negotiate and support. Raising children is a contract to love, encourage, nurture, and build a family. Between employer and employee the contract is for money and work. (It's only recently that the terms "motivation" and "encouragement" have begun to be part of the language of management.) There is a shift in both marriage and management toward the creation of connection and intimacy instead of maintaining the power struggle of adversaries. You may be able to have your way as an employer, but within a marriage and family you need to be able to separate ideal expectations from the performances of real people. You may not be able to have your preference or your version of perfect if the cost to the other persons in the relationship is too high.

> *"Your father doesn't know it yet, but he's going to paint the porch next weekend."*

> *"You're just like your mother."*

> *"You didn't turn out the way I thought you would."*

> *"I'll never forgive you!"*

Depending on your family background, complaining, competing, and criticizing may be the normal pattern of exchange. Some couples bicker constantly as their only way of connecting. They spend their lives in one long verbal power struggle. They attack over money, children, friends, and competence and constantly monitor each other's behavior. They wound deeply, particularly when they uncover a secret insecurity. Imagine that, at the moment of falling in love or making a commitment to each other, they were given a huge red cardboard heart and two single hole punches. Every time they send a barb, a zinger, or a zap to the other person they are punching a hole in the heart. It takes a while for enough of them to accumulate to disintegrate the heart and the love it represents.

*"You're a wussy."*

*"I could have married . . ."*

*"Why am I stuck with you?"*

*"You tell me not to put my feet on the table. Who are you to talk, when you don't even make the bed?"*

*"You're the hardest person in the world to live with."*

*"You might work hard, but there's never enough to pay the bills."*

Husband to wife: *"Thank you for knitting me this sweater."*
Wife to husband: *"I made it big and bulky to cover your fat."*

*"I wouldn't fool around if you* looked *better."*

*"If you really cared about your family, you would buy a better car."*

*"Spendthrift!"*

Wife: *"Honey, you really should fix the leaking pipe in the kitchen."* Later, after Honey has spent two hours under the sink with skinned knuckles and water dripping in his face: *"How are you doing, honey? Perhaps we should call a plumber before you break something."*

These are mild compared to some exchanges between loved ones. All the variations of verbal assaults in this book get used when two people live together. Because criticism stimulates defensive behavior, many couples don't even remember what they said or why they said it. When confronted, they will deny everything. They agree with nothing the other says, marshal other criticisms to rebut previous hurts, repeat all prior criticism of the person, especially ones that have been emotionally successful. These include criticism of friends, relatives, profession, ex-spouses, stepchildren, physical image, and intelligence. And some people even reveal the intimate secrets and weaknesses of their spouses in public.

When confronted with their verbal behavior by a friend, child, or counselor they may defend the entire pattern:

*"You know I wouldn't say this if I didn't love him."*

*"Oh, she didn't mind."*

*"It's just our way of showing we care."*

*"We're being honest."*

*"She knows I don't mean it."*

Honesty can be used as a form of aggression in families because it makes sense; e.g., "I care enough to take the risk of telling you this." You can usually understand the underlying motivation in yourself and others by how you feel when you make a comment or receive one. You will know whether honesty is being used to hurt or help.

We also criticize on an unconscious level. We don't actually say anything, but we withhold attention or approval. The other person gets the message, but because it is never verbalized, there is no chance for him or her to negotiate or solve the problem. Charles Schulz, who draws the "Peanuts" cartoon, found his marriage of twenty-three years ending. "I don't think she liked me anymore," he said simply, "and I just got up and left one day, walked out the door, because I didn't know what to do."

Try to listen to what you and those you care about are actually saying to each other. It can help to tape-record a conversation. You may be stunned at your words and tone of voice. There are books on treating each other with kindness, deepening love and communication, and building intimacy. I've listed some in this book's Bibliography. Check your patterns, review how your parents talked to each other, and decide whether you want to change. There are many gentle, caring ways to tell people what you need to tell them. There are fair ways to negotiate or fight. Here are a few ideas to help you understand what you are doing and why. They may also help you in talking to your friends.

- Decide on your goal. What do you want to change? Or are you just releasing hostility? What is it you're trying to say? What response are you hoping for? Let the other person(s) know specifically what you want.

- Don't just complain. Ask for a reasonable change that will please you.

- What do you know about yourself that might be contributing to the problem? Check your family patterns, anxieties, and self-value. Take time to consult your real feelings.

- What do you know about your partner that would change the way you present a problem? How can you help him or her to feel safe and able to respond?

- Hold each other's hand while you talk, so that there is some love flowing back and forth between you.

- Limit yourself to one issue at a time. Don't dump a lot of gripes or skip back and forth. It's too confusing and too hard to respond to.

- Take a break if you find yourself getting angry and defensive.

- Avoid labels, name-calling, glib remarks, sarcasm, judgments, and intolerance.

- Listen to what the other person has to say before defending yourself—really listen! What's behind a hurtful remark can lead to real understanding.

- Do you want to *increase* or *decrease* the love between you? Always consider compromise. People often have different perceptions of the same reality. You both want to win. The reward is more intimacy.

When we don't communicate in gentle ways, we can slip into destructive silence or emotional numbness. We may feel or mask anger that covers up the hurt. Underneath all these emotions is the fear that we are vulnerable and unlovable.

Keep your love strong by protecting yourself and others from criticism by using the techniques in this book. Don't let relatives or strangers insult your children. Refuse to accept insults under the guise of love. When you are no longer a willing victim or attacker, the whole pattern in your family may change. It will be safe to love.

# Evaluation and Motivation: The Workplace

*"It took you a whole month to do this?"*

*Boss to employee: "This office looks really nice the way you've fixed it up. Don't get used to it."*

*"I can't believe I hired you."*

---

The ability to learn from evaluation on the job, even if it is negative, is an important skill. This is one area in which negative feedback may be important information —if you can make it work for you. Many men learn how early in their life, because of their traditional experiences with coaching. They have some support from other players, so that even with a harsh coach they can learn not to take the criticism as a blow to their own self-esteem. They can separate *task* criticism from *personal* criticism. Men learn strong, silent behavior that conceals their reactions and their feelings. It is a problem in intimate exchanges but useful in any task-oriented setting.

Traditionally, most evaluation of females was not task oriented as much as a comment on appearance or personality. Constant evaluation of one's physical image leaves many women with the feeling that there is something wrong with them. Criticism is therefore almost always felt by women as personal. Combined with this is the cultural permission to express feelings and to display sensitivity: women cry when hurt, men try not to. These differences are changing as our sex roles change, but they may still be a part of our internal reactions.

## *Being Evaluated*

Our sensitivity is also a problem for employers who may not be sophisticated or skilled in communication. Regardless of the style and the personality of your evaluator, an employee *can* control how he or she responds. Here are some ways for you to depersonalize an evaluation process and learn what you need to learn to succeed in most work situations. If you still feel abused, file a grievance or change jobs.

**Avoid being defensive.** Easier said than done, but try listening to criticism as a report. Control your fear. It may be just a difference of opinion. Remember to breathe, relax, gently evaluate yourself as you are being evaluated. Don't personalize, try not to make it an emotional issue, be open to information. If it stings, you have plenty of time to process it alone or with a friend.

**Check your self-esteem.** You need to know your personal history or you will forever repeat your family roles at work. Is this really an attack on your self-worth? Has

this happened to you before? Could you be misunderstanding the intent or process of evaluation?

**Check the source.** Is this person the appropriate one to evaluate you and your performance? Does he or she have power over your position in this company? Who is he or she reporting to? Be sensitive to the work environment you are both in. Is the person who is criticizing you in some bind? If the person is emotional or zealous, someone or something may be pushing him.

**Get enough information.** You may have missed some important points if the conversation has upset you. Make sure you understand what has been said and what is expected of you. Ask for the evaluation in writing. Is it consistent with other reports, or is this a unique or isolated problem? Ask for specific ways to improve. Tell the evaluator you appreciate his help.

**Ask for help.** Who can you turn to for assistance in understanding the evaluation and responding in a professional manner? Would a seminar help? Is there any reading material available?

**Prioritize.** What are the most important and least important elements in the evaluation? Do you think your supervisor would agree with your ordering of these? Break the change down into manageable steps. Move forward, but be patient with yourself.

**Decide what you are willing to do.** Is the change you would have to make to eliminate the criticism worth the energy you will have to expend? How will you benefit? What are you willing to do? What will happen if you do not change? You do not have to keep this job. No one comes to get you in the morning with handcuffs; you have alternatives. List five alternative ways you could earn a living. How you respond to an evaluation is your choice.

**Respond.** Whatever you decide, do respond to your critic so he doesn't conclude that you're ignoring him. You may be able to create a productive dialogue by reconnecting, once you have thought the information through. Most managers can accept disagreement. It is better to negotiate openly than simply to carry on in your own way, disregarding their involvement in the outcome.

## The Helpful Evaluation

Many people in positions of power have little training in effective evaluation. It helps to assume that they are doing the best they can with the limited skills most of us have in providing training, feedback, and a good learning process. The best evaluations will incorporate the following elements:

**Respecting privacy.** Any public attacks on an employee break trust and create the desire to sabotage. A defensive person cannot hear what you are saying. Avoid public criticism, sarcasm, or kidding with a negative tone.

**Clear objectives.** Know what it is that you want to accomplish. What change in performance and what measurements will you use to calculate the success of the process?

**Thoughtfulness.** Frustrated outbursts and gunnysacking (dumping a bunch of criticisms you've been saving for months) don't help anyone. Sensitivity is more motivating.

**Specificity.** General statements like "I don't like your attitude" are hard for anyone to respond to. "I am concerned about your not bringing enough books and pamphlets to the conference" frames a problem that can be discussed. "We want you to do better" is not as helpful as a list of specific areas of responsibility—mail order, accounts, sales—and an evaluation of the perceived level of performance in each. "We expected more from you" deflates an employee with a generalized failure, rather than providing a chance to respond with improvement. The employee needs to know what you prefer and what he or she could have done differently.

**Positiveness.** Reinforce the positive ties between you as well, not just the negative. You want the employee to feel *more* committed, not *less*.

**Promoting understanding.** Let the employee ask questions until you know absolutely that the two of you are talking about the same situation.

**Being professional, not personal.** The issue here is not the basic human worth of the employee, only his or her job skills and performance. You want to concentrate on the problem, not the employee, because you want documentable results.

**Negotiability.** The employee needs some control over the solution and his or her response to your comments. Be open to the employee's ideas about the situation.

**Being process-oriented.** Evaluation is a learning tool and part of a process that will last as long as you two work together. Always schedule another meeting! A review of progress will indicate a continuing relationship and your belief in a positive outcome.

Even with all the possible drawbacks of the process it is far better to work with someone who provides direct feedback than to guess at your success. Next time you change jobs, ask about the evaluation process at the time of your job interview. If you get promoted in your current position, ask about any forthcoming evaluation. The more you know about the "review" philosophy of your employer, the easier it will be to do a good job— and know that you're doing a good job.

# *Epilogue*

Perspective is a crucial element in our happiness and in our willingness to treat others with kindness. This book is intended to ease our interaction with others and add some humor to taking good care of ourselves. We will never be able to stop all the hurtful comments from reaching us. We ourselves will make mistakes in what we say to others. We do the best we can with what we know and with who we are. Forgiveness is probably our most important ability.

Defend yourself when it seems appropriate, but consider adding a ten-percent factor in your life whenever possible. Assume that most people are doing the best they can. Many are simply unaware. *You* are often living your life the same way. We are all far less aware of the impact of our behavior than we need to be. We underestimate, so grace helps.

> Ten percent of the time when you buy something it will turn out to be cheaper somewhere else.
> Ten percent of the time when you split a dinner check you will pay more than your share.
> Ten percent of the time when you lend something to someone it will come back damaged.
> Ten percent of the time in various deals you will get cheated.
> Ten percent of the time even your best friend may say something thoughtless and regret it.

It costs far more to constantly defend, to need to be right, and to be always in control. Grace in your friendships is certainly worth something: It reduces stress, for example. Let grace into your life and it will give you much more than a ten-percent return.

When you travel in another culture or country, allow a twenty-percent grace factor. It takes that much to account for confusion and language barriers. If you think a taxi driver has taken advantage of you, don't ruin your vacation. Just add it to the cost of experiencing the world.

Public grace will reduce tension, improve your perception of life, strengthen your relationships, and increase your joy. You'll end up with more of everything!

# Bibliography

AUGSBURGER, DAVID. *Caring Enough to Confront.* Scottsdale, PA: Herald Press, 1981.

BACH, GEORGE R., and RONALD M. DEUTSCH. *Stop—You're Driving Me Crazy.* New York: Berkley Publishing, 1979.

BANDLER, RICHARD, and JOHN GRINDER. *Frogs into PRINCES.* Moab, UT: Real People Press, 1979.

———. *The Structure of Magic I.* Moab, UT: Real People Press, 1975.

———. *The Structure of Magic II.* Moab, UT: Real People Press, 1976.

BERNHARD, YETTA M. *Self-Care.* Millbrae, CA: Celestial Arts, 1975.

BLANCHARD, MARJORIE, and MARK J. TAGER, M.D. *Working Well*. New York: Simon and Schuster, 1985.

BLOOMFIELD, HAROLD. *Life Mates*. New York: New American Library, 1989.

BRAKER, HARRIET B. *The Type E Woman*. New York: Dodd, Mead, and Co., 1986.

BRANDT, DAVID. *Is That All There Is?* New York: Pocket Books, 1984.

BRIGGS, DOROTHY. *Celebrate Yourself: Enhancing Your Own Self-Esteem*. New York: Doubleday, 1986.

———. *Your Child's Self-Esteem: The Key to His Life*. New York: Doubleday, 1970.

CLARKE, JEAN ILLSEY. *Self-Esteem: A Family Affair*. New York: Harper & Row, 1980.

COHEN, HERB. *You Can Negotiate Anything*. New York: Bantam Books, 1980.

CRARY, ELIZABETH. *Without Spanking or Spoiling: A Practical Approach to Toddler and Preschool Guidance*. Seattle: Parenting Press, 1979.

CROSBY, PHILIP B. *Running Things*. New York: McGraw-Hill, 1986.

CURRAN, DELORES. *Stress and the Healthy Family*. Minneapolis: Winston Press, 1985.

DINKMEYER, DON, and GARY D. McKAY. *The Parent's Handbook: Systematic Training for Effective Parenting*. New York: Random House, 1982.

DURANT, WILL. *The Story of Civilization*. New York: Simon and Schuster, 1935.

ELGIN, SUZETTE HADEN. *The Gentle Art of Verbal Self-Defense*. New York: Dorset Press, 1980.

FABER, ADELE, and ELAINE MAZLISH. *How to Talk So Kids Listen and Listen So Kids Will Talk*. New York: Avon Books, 1985.

FERNSTERHEIM, HERBERT, and JEAN BAER. *Don't Say Yes When You Want to Say No*. New York: Dell Publishing Co., 1975.

FISHER, ROGER, and WILLIAM URY. *Getting to Yes*. New York: Penguin Books, 1983.

FRIEDMAN, MARTHA. *Overcoming the Fear of Success*. New York: Warner Books, 1982.

GEUDLIN, EUGENE T. *Focusing*. New York: Bantam Books, 1981.

GLASS, LILLIAN. *Talk to Win*. New York: Perigee Books, 1987.

GREENING, TOM, and DICK HOBSON. *Instant Relief: The Encyclopedia of Self-Help*. New York: Wideview Books, 1979.

HALPERN, HOWARD. *Cutting Loose: An Adult Guide to Coming to Terms With Your Parents*. New York: Bantam Books, 1978.

HAUCH, PAUL A. *Overcoming Frustration and Anger*. Philadelphia: Westminister Press, 1974.

HUFFINES, LaUNA. *Connecting*. New York: Harper & Row, 1986.

JAMES, JENNIFER. *Life Is a Game of Choice*. Seattle: Bronwen Press, 1986.

———. *Women and the Blues: Passions That Hurt, Passions That Heal*. San Francisco: Harper & Row, 1988.

KRANTZLER, MEL. *Learning to Love Again*. New York: Harper & Row, 1977.

LA ROE, MARLENE SHELTON. *How Not to Ruin a Perfectly Good Marriage*. New York: Bantam Books, 1980.

LEDERER, WILLIAM, and DON JACKSON. *The Mirages of Marriage*. New York: W. W. Norton and Co., 1968.

LEEFELDT, CHRISTINE, and ERNEST CALLENBACH. *The Art of Friendship*. New York: Berkley Books, 1979.

LENZ, ELINOR. *Once My Child . . . Now My Friend*. New York: Warner Books, 1981.

LEONARD, LINDA SCHIERSE. *The Wounded Woman: Healing the Father-Daughter Relationship*. Athens: Ohio University Press, 1982.

LERNER, HARRIET G. *The Dance of Anger: A Woman's Guide to Changing the Patterns of Intimate Relationships*. New York: Harper & Row, 1985.

MANDEL, BOB. *Two Hearts Are Better Than One*. Berkeley, CA: Celestial Arts, 1986.

McGINNIS, ALAN LOY. *Friendship Factor*. Minneapolis: Augsburg Publishing House, 1979.

NEWMAN, MILDRED, and BERNARD BERKOWITZ. *How to Be Your Own Best Friend*. New York: Ballantine Books, 1984.

PEELE, STANTON, and ARCHIE BRODSKY. *Love and Addiction*. New York: Taplinger, 1975.

PHELPS, STANLEE, and NANCY AUSTIN. *The Assertive Woman*. San Luis Obispo, CA: Impact, 1975.

REID, JOHN. *Living with Teenagers: A Survival Manual for Adults*. Everett, WA: Ampersand Publishing, 1983.

ROOSEVELT, RUTH, and JEANETTE LOFAR. *Living in Step*. New York: McGraw-Hill, 1977.

RUBIN, THEODORE. *Compassion and Self-Hate*. New York: Ballantine Books, 1976.

RUSK, TOM, and RANDY READ. *I Want to Change But I Don't Know How*. Los Angeles: Price, Stern, and Sloan Publishers, 1986.

SCHEID, ROBERT. *Beyond the Love Game*. Berkeley, CA: Celestial Arts, 1980.

SHAIN, MERLE. *Some Men Are More Perfect Than Others*. New York: Bantam Books, 1980.

———. *When Lovers Are Friends*. New York: Bantam Books, 1980.

SHEEHY, GAIL. *Spirit of Survival*. New York: William Morrow and Co., 1980.

SMEDES, LEWIS. *Forgive and Forget: Healing the Hurts We Don't Deserve*. San Francisco: Harper & Row, 1984.

VISCOTT, DAVID. *Risking*. New York: Pocket Books, 1977.

VISHER, JOHN AND EMILY. *How to Win as a Stepfamily.* New York: Dembner Books, 1982.

WOITITZ, JANET. *The Struggle for Intimacy.* Pompano Beach, FL: Health Communications, 1985.

# About the Author

Jennifer James, Ph.D., is one of the country's most popular lecturers and the author of seven books including *Visions from the Heart*, *Windows*, and the bestselling *Success Is the Quality of Your Journey*, holds a doctorate in cultural anthropology and master's degrees in both history and psychology. For almost twelve years, she has written a weekly column for the *Seattle Times* and, as one of the area's most popular commentators, hosted a daily talk show that helped people understand psychology, culture, perception, and the choices they are making in their lives. She lectures worldwide to school, university, and professional groups, including ITT, IBM, Boeing, and the Young Presidents' Organization. Dr. James lives in Seattle, Washington.

Jennifer James has helped thousands to change their attitudes from the conventional yardstick of success—and to lead happier, more peace-filled lives. Reward a friend with Dr. James's writings on how to stop the grind and share the moments of pleasure and warmth.

*Visions* In this book of meditations James takes her readers on a step-by-step journey to self-discovery and personal change. Trade paperback. 144 pages.

*Success Is the Quality of Your Journey* 120 insights and ideas on subjects such as risk, solitude, aging, and relationships. Trade paperback. 144 pages.

*Windows* 120 more essays on the topics of day-to-day living, intimacy, heroic acts, traveling (including the author's journey to Nepal), and more. Trade paperback. 160 pages.

*Defending Yourself Against Criticism: The Slug Manual* Filled with nitty-gritty advice for both the giver and getter of criticism, James's book will help readers defend themselves from—and laugh at—the absurd and harmful things we say to each other. Illustrated. Trade paperback. 144 pages.

Ask for these titles at your local bookstore, or order by mail today.

Use this coupon, or write to:
Newmarket Press, 18 East 48th Street, New York, NY 10017

Please send me:

_____copies of *Visions*, in paperback, @ $9.95 each;

_____copies of *Success*, in paperback, @ $9.95 each;

_____copies of *Windows*, in paperback, @ $9.95 each;

_____copies of *Defending Yourself Against Criticism*, in paperback, @ $9.95 each.

Please include applicable sales tax, and add $2.00 for postage and handling (plus $1.00 for each additional item ordered)—check or money order only. Please allow 4-6 weeks for delivery. Prices and availability are subject to change.

Enclosed is a check or money order, payable to Newmarket Press, in the amount of $_____.

Name _____

Address _____

City/State/Zip _____

Companies, professional groups, clubs, and other organizations may qualify for special terms on quantity purchases of these titles. For more information, please phone or write: Special Sales Department, Newmarket Press, 18 East 48th Street, New York, N.Y. 10017 (212) 832-3575.

jj993.pm4